A Bountiful Heart
The Life of Bob Evans

By Robbin Evans
With Mike Harden

Preface from the works of Wendell Berry

A Bountiful Heart
The Life of Bob Evans

By Robbin Evans
With Mike Harden

ISBN No. 978-0-615-23523-3

Garden Flower is a copyrighted poem of Anthony Donskov
It is used here with permission of the author

Table of Contents

Acknowledgements

Among the many people who made this book a reality, none deserves more gratitude than my mother. I cannot thank her enough for sharing memories of a man whose loss was still so fresh to her—indeed, to all of us. Dozens of kin and friends lent their memories and words to the telling of my father's story. I would be remiss if I did not thank my siblings—sister Debbie and brothers Stan, Steve and Bobby. Dad's grandchildren were most generous with their time. Matt, Misha and Anthony Donskov, sons of my sister Debbie and her husband Paul Donskov were most gracious. Bart Kayser, my late sister Gwen's son, shared many recollections. I thank my daughter Alex for a storehouse of reminiscences as well as the foreword to this book. My son Max had much to offer about dad and a great deal of creative input. Although my father outlived many of his contemporaries, there were several voices from his early years that strengthened the book in many ways. First and foremost, I want to thank dad's best friend and close colleague, Harold Cregor and his wife Marevia, along with Herb and Pauline Bush, Elmer Hill, Frankie Burke, Buzz Call and Forrest "Putzig" Clark. The story of dad's years at Greenbrier Military School would have been difficult to recount without the voices of Joe Lemon, George Lemon and Herb Pearis. From dad's early years in starting up Bob Evans Restaurants, I relied heavily upon the collective memories of Roger Williams, Bob Wood, Howard Berry, Richard "Mac" McLaren and Larry Corbin. Telling the story of my father's long involvement with Quarter Horses was much easier thanks to Nancy Folck, Leo "Pee Wee" Barbera, Clark Bradley, Ed Dingledine and the staff of the Ohio Quarter Horse Association. Professor David Zartman recounted dad's unswerving crusade on behalf of year-round grazing, along with Indiana farmer Dave Forgey who, for years, has made it a practice at his farm. Horse trainer Bill Wells recalled the adventures involved in dad's efforts to spare the once-endangered Spanish-Barb mustangs. Neal Orth, Katherine Harsh and Randy Reed were central to the passages in this book that deal with dad's Charolais cattle. Kenny Tomlinson and Bob Donnet were wellsprings of information about my father's conservation efforts. Dr. George Wolfe and Mary Lee Marchi assisted greatly in recounting how the Homestead became a tour destination for hundreds of thousands of visitors. Brenda Haas, Neomi White and Regina Webb play an indispensable role in dad's devotion to seeing that Appalachian high school scholars realize their dreams of attending college. The story of one of those students, Jill Sullivan, can be found in this book's introduction. I thank her for sharing it, because the good works of the Ohio Appalachian Center for Higher Education was uppermost among the defining passions of dad's life and will be a beneficiary of this book's sales. To that end, I am also grateful to members of the corporate staff of Bob Evans Farms, in particular CEO Steve Davis, Mary Cusick and Sarah Porter. I thank, as well, for the generous sharing of his time and his considerable skills as a cardiologist, the good Dr. Brian Griffin. I cannot express the depth of my gratitude for the voice of author, poet, farmer and sage Wendell Berry. He and my father were twin sons of different mothers, and his eloquence gives voice to my father's deepest beliefs. Finally, I offer thanks to good friend Louise Suttmiller for her invaluable support and wise counsel as I worked to tell my father's story.

FOR MY FATHER,

The visionary, the dreamer, the believer,

The "unmoved mover."

He had the courage to follow his dreams

And the breadth and generosity of character

To lead those around him to do the same.

He refused to be defined by others.

And, throughout his life,

He continued to pursue missions

Greater than himself

In order to effect the improvement of the community,

Of youth, of farming and, of his neighbors

In an attempt "to leave the world a bit better."

AND TO THE MEMORY OF MY SISTER, GWEN

Special Thanks To

Dr. John Sena,
Professor Emeritus of English at
The Ohio State University
friend & mentor

Kay Halasek
my editor

Marjorie Evans
a lifetime family friend

and, Mike.

Remembering My Father
By Wendell Berry

What did I learn from him?
He taught the difference
Between good work and sham,
Between nonsense and sense.

He taught me sentences,
Outspoken fact for fact,
In swift coherences
Discriminate and exact.

He served with mind and hand
What we were hoping for:
The small house on the land,
The shade tree by the door,

Garden, smokehouse, and cellar,
Granary, crib, and loft
Abounding, and no year
Lived at the next year's cost.

He kept in mind, alive,
The idea of the dead:
"A steer should graze and thrive
Wherever he lowers his head."

He said his father's saying.
We were standing on the hill
To watch the cattle grazing
As the gray evening fell.

"Look. See that this is good,
And then you won't forget."
I saw it as he had,
And I have not forgot.

Preface

From the works of Wendell Berry

The streams and the woods don't care if you love them. The place (farm)
doesn't care if you love it. But for your own sake you had better love it.
For the sake of all else you love, you had better love it.

Hannah Coulter by
Wendell Berry

The words of Wendell Berry, author, essayist, poet, farmer and steward of the land, speak with elegant simplicity of my father's dreams. Dad was genuinely humbled by the gift outright of earth. He never surrendered the hope that it might one day be restored to a family-based, responsibly managed method of agricultural production that could sustain the small farmer as well as provide his offspring with an alternative to fleeing to the nearest metropolis for a city job.

Berry writes with passion for such hopes. The Earth endures and fulfills its promise to us, the Bible states, though we have sullied that bequest from the heavens and, in the process, given a hostage to posterity against the birthright of our children. My father fought the good fight for a method of year-round grazing that would have allowed the small cattle farmer to run his business with nothing more than one tractor and minimal storage of winter silage.

So much of what my father believed of our indebtedness to the soil and our responsibility to posterity made him a man of like mind and kindred heart to all that Berry believes, and of which he wrote with passion and profundity.

Wendell Berry has been kind enough to lend to my father's story some of those words, those thoughts—some ringing with the urgency of a firebell in the night—that call us to our duty to make things better. Berry brings a rare insight to the credo that became my father's mission: The idea that we are obliged to spend our brief season upon this earth as vigilant and dedicated stewards of the land that has sustained us.

In his books, The Gift of Good Land, We Have Begun and Hannah Coulter, Berry reminds us of how family farming is sealing its own fate by turning away from the old ways and succumbing to a debt-driven reliance on egregiously high-priced farm equipment and skyrocketing fuel prices that line only the pockets of the corporate hierarchy of oil and farm machinery manufacturing companies. He articulates with quiet fury those which were the deepest convictions of my father:

And so we see that, though our agriculture may use relatively little fossil fuel energy, it is almost totally dependent on what it does use. It uses fossil fuel energy almost exclusively and uses it in competition with other users. And the sources of this energy are not renewable.

This critical dependence on nonrenewable energy sources is the direct result of the industrialization of agriculture. Before industrialization, agriculture depended almost exclusively on solar energy. Solar energy not only grew the plants, as it still does, but also provided the productive power of farms in the form of the work of humans and animals. This energy is derived and made available biologically, and it is recyclable. It is inexhaustible in the topsoil so long as good husbandry keeps the life cycle intact.

The old sun-based agriculture was fundamentally alien in the industri-

al economy; industrial corporations could make relatively little profit from it. In order to make agriculture fully exploitable by industry it was necessary (in Barry Commoner's terms) to weaken "the farm's link to the sun and to make the farmland a "colony" of the industrial corporations. The farmers had to be persuaded to give up the free energy of the sun in order to pay dearly for the machine-derived energy of fossil fuels.

Such farming was traditional here. It was not uniformly good, and it had not solved all of its problems, but it was in many ways admirable. It could have been built upon and improved. We did not build upon it and improve it. Instead, we have allowed it to be nearly destroyed by the methods and the economy of industrialization...The old subsistence economy is virtually extinct.

Thus we have another example of a system artificially expanded for profit. The farm's originally organic, coherent, independent production system was expanded into a complex dependence on remote sources and on manufactured supplies.

What happened, from a cultural point of view, was that machines were substituted for farmers, and energy took the place of skill. As farmers became more and more dependent on fossil fuel energy, a radical change occurred in their minds. Once focused on biology, the life and health of living things, their thinking now began to focus on technology and economics. Credit, for example, became as pressing an issue as the weather, for farmers had begun to climb the one-way ladder of survival by debt. Bigger machines required more land, and more land required yet bigger machines, which required yet more land, and on and on—the survivors climbing to precarious and often temporary success by way of machines and mortgages and the ruin of their neighbors. And so, the farm became a "factory" where speed, "efficiency," and profitability were the main standards of performance. These standards, of course, are industrial, not agricultural.

The final irony is that we are abusing our land in this way partly in order to correct our "balance of payments"—that is, in order to buy foreign petroleum. In the language of some "agribusiness" experts we are using "agri-dollars" to offset the drain of petro-dollars." We are, in effect, exporting our topsoil in order to keep our tractors running.

There is no question that you can cover a lot of ground with the big machines now on the market. A lot of people seem entranced by the power and speed of those machines, which the manufacturers love to refer to as "monsters" and "acre eaters." But the result is not farming; it is a process closely akin to mining. In what is left of the country communities, in earshot of the monster acre eaters of the "agri-businessmen," a lot of old farmers must be turning over in their graves.

The reason is simply that we have learned, and become willing, to market and use up in our own time the birthright and livelihood of posterity.

To survive, our farmers are going to need a fully developed local land-based economy supported by informed and locally-committed urban consumers. To achieve this will require a long time and a lot of work, but we have begun.

Foreword

Alex Chamberlain

Granddaughter

As a young girl, I was fortunate to spend the most formative years of my life in a place of incomparable heart. Southern Ohio was a place where dirt roads cut through green rolling hills, farms marked the way, and creeks and ponds offered the perfect afternoon escape. The easy tenor of voice and cadence of speech was as common as the outstretched hand and congenial welcome. You understood that, even in very few words, much was shared. It was a place where pleasantries carried genuine interest and family matters mattered. It was a community of kind people living and acknowledging all around them. It was a beautiful place to be, and those feelings I carry to this day. This book has been written as a tribute to the life of my grandfather, a man who embodied all of these sentiments and, I believe, infused them with his own passion and enthusiasm.

I had never recognized energy quite like his. Even at the age of 6, I knew it was inimitable. You could hear it in the doorknob even before he entered the room. He was a juggernaut, a whirlwind of ideas coming to action with each step. He was "a visionary on parade." His wholehearted personality and generosity of spirit fit him better than his Stetson and string tie. I think the only thing that ever stopped him in his tracks was my grandma.

The round kitchen table in my grandparents' home was a place of many meals for my brother and me. It was a constant hub of action: phones ringing, people coming and going, stopping in to say hello and to share a story or something from their farm or garden. All the while, timers signaled for pies to be pulled from the oven, pots boiled on the stove and the smells of the out-of-doors mingled with the home-cooked food my grandma prepared. Throughout my life, I found that it would be hard to find a meal, even in the whitest of table-clothed restaurants, that plated a better-tasting spread than my grandma. And, it was on one of those days, sitting at that table in the middle of chaos, that I remembered looking at my grandfather, a sideways glance through the half-circle bite of my bologna sandwich, and being mesmerized.

His stubbled chin and cheeks, always flush with pink, pinched in the corners of his eyes when he smiled and talked, and he was always doing one, the other or both. He spoke big, with an excited voice that implied that he "was onto something" and willing to share whatever he knew with whomever was smart enough to listen. He was like watching a story unfold and, as a young girl, there was nothing better.

Half the time I wasn't really sure where he was going or why, but I knew it would be fun. Along the way, we would surely stop to talk to a couple of people about matters of which I knew nothing, but which would be resolved with a smack on the hood of his truck and my grandpa's three-finger wave. A part for some piece of farm equipment would either be ready to pick up or drop off at the supply store. We would visit someone else's barn, home or business, stop to kick the tires and be on our way. There was never a trip when I wouldn't have to get out and unchain a gate and re-lock it. We drove through rutted pasture fields and scaled steep hillsides that even the bravest of Chevy ad-men wouldn't dare tout as possible. We dragged dead logs and thicket to burn piles, clearing land for the cattle. I often found myself in the middle of a multiflora rose bush, cutting and pruning it down to its demise. I must have really liked him to do all that. And, I did. And, most times, at the end of our trip or somewhere along the way, we were met by the broad, white faces of his Charolais cattle. Bovine who were, no doubt, not surprised to see his blue pickup. He would check that they had successfully been moved from one pasture to the next, eating fresh grass while the adjoining field replenished itself for their eventual return. He tended to them and his land, as he did to everything he loved, with dogged devotion.

To most people, my grandfather was a successful entrepreneur and this, of course, is true. He worked for years building bridges and breaking barriers that existed in the restaurant and food industry. He worked tirelessly, creating a company that represented a haven for weary travelers and hungry families; a place that was worthy of carrying his name. He lived by the belief that quality was not just spoken about but carried through in every detail of business, from product to relationship. With each deliberate step he took, he knew that he was creating something much bigger than himself. He was not looking for fortune or fame, rather he had an enormous appetite for the challenges, for the generation of ideas and the possibilities that would come and eventually outlast him and all who read this book. His success was founded in more than gumption and fortitude. It came from the soil on the bottom of his shoes, the faces of his neighbors, the hills that he was so proud to call home.

The greatest thing my grandfather ever did was never leaving where he came from and never forgetting why. He found the most profoundly beautiful of all things right there in the valleys of southern Ohio—my grandmother, the land of Gallia County, his family, his friends and his farm. Looking back over the years, I realize that he never wanted or needed anything more than home. And, it was a home that he, even to his final days, helped to create. Sometimes, as with a willful teenager, he had to use his judgment and be patient with the process; but he never, not even at the darkest hour, gave up on home. He believed more in his community and the people it embraced than himself, than in almost anything. He fought for the underdog every time, but he did so because he knew that, against all odds, there was always a chance. I have yet to meet anyone with this ability and, even as a young girl, I recognized his unabashed love and appreciation for people. He was connected to these things foremost because they resonated within him like the call of wild geese or even a gentle April rain; he knew them well but loved them more.

I don't think, when he started making sausage, that he ever knew the magnitude of success it would create, not only by Wall Street standards, but also in the lives he touched. I think he wanted to make a superior product and sell it with an honest handshake in hopes of beginning a new and lasting friendship. This was never clearer to me than after his death. The sheer number of people who visited his calling hours was staggering. Not one person, to my knowledge, left early without paying respects to him, my grandmother and the family, even though the line stretched up one hallway and down another, out the door and down the steps into the heat and humidity of a June afternoon. At times these people stood for hours, talking amongst themselves, perusing photographs from his life and articles that decorate the walls of Bob Evans Hall at the University of Rio Grande. Some had worked at various restaurants together; some held pictures and snapshots taken years back with my grandfather at a restaurant opening or at the Ohio State Fair. All of them were personally and profoundly grateful for the life he had led and the opportunities that he created in their lives. I heard, more than once, the humble voices of fellow Ohioans and Midwesterners expressing to my grandmother, "Bob Evans helped put my son through school." Or, "Bob gave me a job when no one else would." All of them were teary-eyed and bewildered by his loss. He meant so much to Ohio, and with each face that passed and walked back out into the heat, I felt their love, respect and gratitude for his life and his legacy.

Throughout my life, I have used my grandparents as models of the person that I aspire to be one day. I learned through them both, through their love, that the most beautiful things in life are simple; that an entire world exists in a blossoming dogwood tree; that each creature, no matter the size, has a purpose; and, that beauty is everywhere. To my grandfather, there was nothing more beautiful than my grandmother. She was his confidante, his shoulder of respite and his beacon. In his final days, the entire Evans family was stricken with grief and overwhelming sadness. I know that this was true of my grandmother, but she held more composure than us all. Maybe it was because she knew the best of my grandfather and shared in all of his life: good and bad. She held his hand in the front seat of his truck from their first date to now, over 67 years later, having never let go. The two of them, being best friends and lovers, created their entire lives around and with each other, knowing that no matter the struggle or joy, they had been side by side. And, throughout our long stays at various hospitals, my grandmother added elegance and beauty to every hallway she strode, each elevator she entered and in each room she graced. Never would she take a wheelchair, but rather, she walked like I imagine the young woman my grandfather fell in love with, down miles of florescent-lit hospital hallways, every moment willing my grandpa to return home.

I guess you could say that he had "beaten death" so many times that I was beginning to think that the Grim Reaper had decided to write him off as a bad prospect. Perhaps Death itself was in awe of his resilience. So, although he was very ill, I was surprised at his death. To me, it was unimaginable. By his sheer nature, by his own generous heart and resolute will, he taught me more about life than anyone. I am eternally grateful.

At your grave I wanted so much to be alone with you just one more time. Even if the moments were filled with silence. Just having you there gave me strength and affirmation that life, even wildly juxtaposed with farm to fame, could still balance perfectly in all its beautiful chaos.

Introduction

William Faulkner said that, perhaps, after death, we become "radio waves," and I can stand here in some preternatural stillness amid the elms and junipers and magnolias and absorb everything of these people I once knew. I return here whenever I can, for there is a lot of sky here, and quiet, and its familiar stones and its sloping hills...fill me with stability.

Willie Morris
North Toward Home

The patch of my father's beloved Gallia County he now occupies at the edge of a high hill above the winding Ohio River is a commanding site whose vista embraces a landscape on which he spent more than 80 years. To the east, upriver, reside the two locations that made up his earliest ventures--the malt shop and the Steak House that he launched in the 1940s, bookends bracketing his World War II Army service guarding German and Italian POWs.

The view to the south might inspire an amusing tale about his days of running bootleg sausage into West Virginia to mom-and-pop stores and restaurants. An over-the-shoulder glance to the north invites a moment of quiet introspection, for within the range of that compass point a thousand memories grew from seed to sapling to shade. Some of my father's hardest-earned achievements were notched there. The old Homestead is now a museum to all the benchmarks and milestones of his life, his career and the family that made it all worthwhile. Portions of the land my father tended remain overgrown with thicket and bramble--sanctuaries where he hunted wild turkey and quail, pastures where his Charolais grazed and headstrong Spanish-Barb mustangs pranced the paddocks. It is the place from which he introduced the world to a "down on the farm" product that became a mealtime staple across the U.S. It is the location, as well, of the Sausage Shop that became the prototype for the familiar red and white Bob Evans Restaurant.

The territory west of my father's gravesite offers less in the way of memories of his life than a metaphor for its meaning. There, the Ohio River curls steadily away from home country. More than 200 years before my dad's passing, that wild old river brought the star-crossed French to a place they would christen, with a mixture of rue and resignation, Gallipolis, the city of Gauls. The Ohio kept right on rolling after those first settlers stepped off of their flatboats. It continued flowing after the Welsh followed the French. As one generation handed the reins to the next, the river flowed and overflowed as it carried the commerce of a young growing land on down to the Mississippi. It dumped memory and silt, triumph and heartache into the Gulf of Mexico from whence Gallia County farmers would await its return on the weatherman's promise that "moisture from the Gulf" would be moving up through the Ohio Valley to slake parched furrows and fields. The western view from my father's grave makes sense of it all. The cycle is complete, yet without end.

"Full circle," dad was fond of saying in his down-home shorthand when searching for a way to convey the inter-connectedness of all that breathes. In Thornton Wilder's play *Our Town*, the narrator invokes that belief when he tells the audience:

Now there are some things we all know, but we don't take'm out and look at'm very often. We all know that something is eternal. And it ain't

houses and it ain't names, and it ain't earth, and it ain't even the stars....
everybody knows in their bones that something is eternal, and that some-
thing has to do with human beings. All the greatest people ever lived have
been telling us that for five thousand years and yet you'd be surprised how
people are always losing hold of it. There's something way down deep
that's eternal about every human being.

At my father's memorial service, a young occupational therapy assistant who had worked with dad at Holzer Hospital in the waning months
of his life rose to recount the story of a connection with dad that had been
absolutely vital to the path she chose in life.

"I'm going to try my hardest not to get too emotional," Jill Sullivan
said as she stepped to the lectern at Ohio State University's Mershon Auditorium and looked out upon those assembled there. A product of a lean
pocket of Lawrence County, she was slightly intimidated by the throng
that had turned out to celebrate dad's life and uncertain whether she could
give breath to her connection with my father without breaking down.

"There I go," she choked. "I cry every time I think about what Bob and
Jewell Evans did for me. I was going to high school in Coal Grove. I had a
lawn service. I was babysitting. I was shoveling horse manure for people. I
didn't have the money to go to school at all."

Unsure of where she might find the funds to pay for tuition, Jill appealed to a friend of my father's and one of the best friends students of
Appalachia ever had--Wayne White. He gave her the money to pay for two
quarters of tuition at Shawnee State. She took it from there and, in early
2007, applied her skills to the recuperation of the man who had helped
author her scholarship. While dad was a patient at Holzer, Sullivan read
an article in the Gallipolis newspaper about his generous help to young
scholars in his home country.

"I learned that the money I had received had initially come from Bob
Evans," Jill told the gathering. "The next morning–Bob was an early
riser–I went into his room. He liked to work with me at about 5:30. I said,

'Buddy, you've gotta get up. We've gotta talk.' I said, 'Bob, do you see what I'm doing here with you today? You did this. Your money sent me to college.'

"I didn't know Bob before then to know if he was an emotional person, but he had tears streaming down his cheeks. He could understand what you were saying to him, but sometimes he had trouble getting out what he wanted to say. He said, 'Full circle. Full circle. Full circle.' Three times."

In that moment, what became clear to Jill Sullivan is something that I have always understood about my father. Though an entrepreneur most commonly celebrated for his achievements in the restaurant and sausage-making business, he was first and foremost a mentor to others. Jill Sullivan was a tree he cultivated unaware that it might provide the most generous of shade in his last days. That was my father.

Full circle. Full circle. Full circle.

Chapter 1
"No Beer. Just Fine Food."

If one advances confidently in the direction of his dreams and endeavors to live the life which he has imagined, he will meet with a success unexpected in common hours.

Henry David Thoreau

The Terminal Steak House, in Gallipolis, never would have made the cover of *Architectural Digest*. A squat, brick-fronted eatery slathered in whitewash, it afforded diners only a dozen stools served by waitresses with names like Dot and Pauline, Velma and Rosa. A jukebox featured the latest love laments of Ernest Tubb and Kitty Wells. Not far up the road from the place, a billboard, my father's lone concession to advertising, caught the eyes of road-weary truckers as the gears groaned and their bellies growled. "No beer. Just Fine Food." And cheap, to boot.

"Ground beef steak, French fries and a salad for 85 cents," remembered Herb Bush, dad's partner in the business. "At lunch, people would be four deep lined up behind the stools waiting to eat." A dime would get you a cup of coffee. A fat slice of homemade pie went for 20 cents. A hamburger fetched a quarter.

In 1946, Route 35, intersecting with the river road along the Ohio, carried a non-stop procession of tractor trailers. They hauled new cars south from Detroit, cigarettes north from the Carolinas to Chicago. Babies weren't the only thing booming in the aftermath of World War II. Peace-time production of domestic goods skyrocketed once factories went from making bombs to baby buggies. A brisk business in home-construction materials fueled a housing explosion. All of it required trucks. A truck terminal adjacent the Steak House offered fuel and maintenance for the rigs while the restaurant provided their drivers with a counter on which to rest their elbows, a comfort-food meal and a waitress who called people "Hon," as in "More coffee for you, Hon?"

At the time he ran that little Steak House, dad was fresh home from a stint in the Army. A little older than many of those trading uniforms for civilian clothes, in 1946 dad was a 28-year-old father of three. Prior to the Army, he had dipped a toe in the restaurant business when he bought half-interest in a malt shop a few miles away from the Steak House. The price was zero down and $500 every six months against a total of $3300. After the war, he sold his 50 percent ownership in the place to the co-proprietor and moved down the road to launch the Steak House.

"That Steak House was a gold mine," recalled dad's longtime friend and first employee, Harold Cregor. It was open 24-7, closing only on Christmas so the employees could spend the holiday with family. Although the Steak House was popular with the locals in Gallipolis, the backbone of the business was truckers. Hauling double-decker loads of a half-dozen new cars down from Detroit, they had no choice but to stop at the truck terminal next to the restaurant--the weight limitations on West Virginia highways forced them to unload half of the cars they were carrying at the terminal, then haul the balance to waiting auto dealerships in Charleston, Huntington and points south. A second driver would pick up the three new cars left at the terminal and proceed into West Virginia. It was time-consuming, and chances were better than average that, at some point in the process, their stomachs would tell them it was time for a break.

Even into my father's late eighties, the imprinted memory of the first menu permitted him to recite, "Ham, two eggs, toast and coffee: 65 cents. Two pork chops, potato salad and a drink for 70 cents. Think of that."

At the time dad opened the Steak House on Eastern Avenue in 1946, he was a relative novice in food service. The malt shop encompassed the total breadth of his experience, yet he knew a little something about customer service and merchandising through his experience with his father Stanley's grocery business. And, if dad was a newcomer to the game, so were many others.

Two decades before dad opened the Steak House, Howard Deering Johnson, a 27-year-old Massachusetts entrepreneur, borrowed $500 and converted a patent-medicine store into a soda shop serving three flavors of ice cream (25 varieties less than his orange-roofed restaurants would boast once the chain went nationwide). A few years before Howard Johnson's opened for business, Billy Ingram, an insurance salesman, partnered with a fry cook named Walt Anderson to start a five-stool burger joint in Wichita, Kansas called White Castle. Those men weren't classmates at the Culinary Institute of America. They were simply men who, like my father, possessed a particular blend of traits; a wonderful mixture comprised of equal parts of resourcefulness, initiative, persistence and vision which served all of them in good stead.

"Dad always saw way down the road," my sister Debbie said of our father.

"He always had a thousand ideas rolling around in his head," Harold Cregor agreed.

"While he was in the Army," my mother Jewell said, "he was continually figuring things out about how he was going to operate that Steak House–what the burgers should weigh, what to charge, what the margin should be. He was sharpening his pencil. Bob was clever. There was a fire burning in there that never went out." Somehow, the computer hard drive that was my father's mind had been wired in an unconventional, perhaps idiosyncratic, yet marvelously astonishing manner. And, as my mother knew only too well, that computer mind of his had no "log off" switch. It ran continually and on very little sleep.

Still, gumption, grit and a head filled with a thousand ideas will get a person only so far in the restaurant business. Dad was also possessed of an amazing knack for engaging people.

"He'd meet people," Debbie observed, "strangers, and embrace their company as though they were neighbors. He met a lot of people that way, and it opened doors. It wasn't about telling people who he was. He simply was able to make himself comfortable in the company of others.

"We would be camping, on a family outing, in a parking lot, anywhere. He would make some small connection. Maybe he would notice an Ohio license tag or a bumper sticker from a vacation attraction we were about to visit." Part of that was a homegrown gregariousness reflective of the era. Whatever it was, wherever its roots, it helped make the Steak House a place to which the truckers returned time and again.

When you're hungry, atmosphere is a poor substitute for mashed potatoes, but when it comes to customer satisfaction, a little bit of friendliness is more valuable than gold. Dad routinely reminded us of that, saying, "'Thank you' doesn't cost a penny. Be sure to thank your customers and tell them you hope they'll visit again soon." It was the gospel of gratitude, and it worked wonders.

"I've seen people standing shoulder to shoulder in that Steak House waiting to get a stool to eat," Harold Cregor said. The 12-stool diner went through more than a thousand ground beef patties each weekend and was doing a stunning business.

A man cut from a different bolt of cloth than my father might have been content to have that little Steak House–thriving and prosperous–represent his chief success in life. That wasn't dad. Challenges energized him, though, once a challenge was successfully surmounted, he had little inclination to sit back and relax. He liked to move on, to solve other problems, to seek another mountain to climb.

Probably more than anything, necessity, the proverbial mother of invention, took a strong hand in directing dad to his next challenge. Although, by the mid-point of the 20th century, the restaurant business in United States was on the cusp of major change, innovation and re-invention. Certain eating habits of the general public remained rather immutable. Sausage, in that day, was a seasonal meat. Because of limited refrigeration, farmers who home-butchered didn't begin making sausage until after the first frost. Sausage, customarily, was also a breakfast-only meat. Yet, to the truckers who frequented dad's Steak House, breakfast time was dictated more by appetite and inclination than the conventions of Eastern Standard Time. Truckers are inveterate breakfast eaters, in part because breakfast has always been the one meal in three required to be both appealing, delicious and functional. A hearty breakfast was regarded as a source of energy for the day ahead. Truckers, wrestling 18-wheelers cross country before interstate highways or power steering, carried big appetites with them. Unfortunately, finding good quality sausage to satisfy those appetites was no easy feat. A diner who ordered sausage in the 1940s had about as much chance of finding lean pork as a man opening a cheap can of pork 'n beans. But, dad simply wouldn't put a product of such low quality on the plates of his diners. He always believed that the most expensive way for a restaurant to get rid of bad food was to serve it to a customer.

He knew a thing or two about meat-cutting from spending time at his uncle's meat-packing business. And, his good buddy Cregor helped out.

The first sausage-making took place in a concrete-block structure not much larger than a two-car garage. My grandfather had agreed to loan his son the money for the building with the provision that extra-wide doors be fitted at each end of the place so it could be used for farm machinery if the business went belly up. It wasn't exactly a vote of confidence, but true to my grandfather Stan's Welsh blood, he was a pragmatist.

A conundrum arose when it came to the matter of christening the new venture. Harold recalled of that discussion, "The place where we were making the sausage was near the tiny town of Evergreen. So, I said, 'Bob, why don't we just call it Evergreen Farm Sausage?' He didn't think that it was too good an idea to have the image of the word *green* attached to any kind of meat you were trying to sell. We settled on Springfield Farm Sausage because we were in Springfield Township."

Everything about the first sausage plant was basic and similar to other such operations everywhere with one major exception.

"At that time," dad said, "pretty much everyone making sausage was using the scraps. It was of such poor quality that sometimes people referred to it as 'bloodshot lard,' which is pretty much what is was. We decided that we were going to use better cuts, hams and tenderloins. People swore that would put us out of business." People were accustomed to an inferior product.

Dad knew that if he was going to compete against cheaper sausage, he was going to have to turn out a product that not only looked remarkable, but which also possessed an exceptional, down-home flavor. Given the unflattering image of sausage in that day, dad and Harold were like a pair of alchemists calculating the best way to make gold. They tinkered with the seasonings, looking for the proper blend of sage and pepper. Both had grown up eating sausage or sausage gravy on hot biscuits, so they knew the precise flavor they were seeking. They fried and tasted repeatedly, even consulting with what my father has described as "the best taste buds in America": his wife, my mother Jewell.

"Dad and mom started this company with nothing, from scratch," my brother Stephen noted. "When dad first got into business, sausage was a low-quality product. The whole essence of what he was trying to do was to make great quality country sausage and put a name on it people could depend on."

When the finished product went on the menu at the Steak House, it immediately climbed to the top of the menu. Truckers, widely regarded in that era as the poor man's restaurant critics, couldn't get over the flavor. This wasn't meat scraps with sage thrown in, a product drowning in its own grease. It was lean, tasty comfort food, pure and simple. The truckers, in their pride of discovery, wanted to take it home for the family table, and dad was only too happy to oblige them. Bulk sausage in tins of five and ten pounds quickly began making it to far-flung points on the road map; the homes of big-rig drivers. At the same time, dad and Harold hit the road, introducing their new product to grocers in West Virginia and Ohio. Harold loaded up his 1946 Studebaker truck with large tins and smaller cloth bags of sausage and headed out for the hills of southern Ohio or the hollows of northern West Virginia, running on "a shoestring and a smile." He made 42 cents an hour, plus 6 cents a mile for gas and wear and tear. "Our motto," he once told a reporter, "was, 'If you wouldn't eat it or take it home to your family, don't pack it.'"

My father and Harold made sausage on Mondays and Thursdays, delivering it next-day fresh to groceries and restaurants. Tales of the running battle dad waged with the state of West Virginia have become the stuff of legend. According to the fine print in the Mountain State's law books, dad's sausage, though superior to anything in the region, was supposed to be inspected before being brought into the state. By contrast, another sub-chapter of the legalese permitted a farmer to bring 12 hogs a year across the state line. Dad preferred the latter provision, arguing that he was, in fact, bringing hogs across the state line. He was just bringing them across in 1-pound bags. Long after law yielded to reason, my father treasured the threatening letter sent to him by a West Virginia bureaucrat hinting darkly that incarceration might be in the picture if he didn't stop peddling in places like Pocatalico and Nitro, Harmony and Frazier's Bottom.

Despite the minor distraction, dad clearly realized that something big was happening. Something good was riding on the wind. But, he and Harold were simply too busy to notice that they were surfing the curl of an enormous wave, a wave that was bigger than both of their imaginations together, and that what they were doing was going to flourish and prosper beyond their wildest beliefs. By grit, wits and elbow grease, my father was forging an early triumph in his life. I was too young to know back then what he thought about his success when he got up in the morning and looked back at the man shaving in the mirror. He wasn't a guy to dwell much on his achievements. A man could get pretty twisted up by suddenly fancying himself the center of the universe. And, besides, dad was too busy moving on to the next project. Time was simply too precious to waste on pride.

The year after the Steak House was launched, dad opened a drive-in restaurant directly next to it. Its first structure was more like a hot dog stand than the curb-service and car-hop business it was soon to become. He was fortunate it didn't float away in the spring of 1948 when the rain-swollen Ohio spilled its banks, dumping a foot of water in the Steak House and making an island of the drive-in. Undaunted, he pushed on, determined to make the drive-in a going proposition. He was good at sorting trends from fleeting fads, and it was clear to him that the motoring public was sold on the idea of eating in the car.

Drive-ins had been around since the 1920s, the term "car hop" having derived from eager servers jumping onto the running boards of automobiles as they eased into a restaurant's serving stalls. In postwar America, with the rationing of gasoline and rubber gone, the nation's love affair with the automobile was in full swing once again. The drive-in was a natural for teens looking for an economical and informal place to congregate. Dad and Herb Bush brainstormed a menu for the place that included a pair of signature sandwiches–the Dutch Boy and the Dutch Girl. The former was a double cheeseburger on three layers of bun. The latter, a single cheeseburger. Fries, shakes and Cokes rounded out the most popular menu items. The Dutch Boy was the best sandwich I have ever eaten. Although dad hand-picked his own top-quality beef, he said that the magic was in the sauce he created. It was similar to, though better than, that used on a Big Mac.

Next door, the homey little Steak House thrived. Strange though it may seem, customers actually purchased postcards of the scene six decades after the place first opened its doors featuring a photo of the restaurant back then. "Wish-you-were-here" messages posted to scattered kin and friends were scribbled beneath a thumbnail description of the spot where they had just dined:

The most modern equipped restaurant in southeastern Ohio, known for its fine food, excellent service and congenial environment. Located at the edge of the historic city of Gallipolis, Ohio, boyhood home of O.O. McIntyre, world's greatest columnist.

Herb Bush managed the Steak House and the drive-in. My father tried to control the skyrocketing sausage business. By early 1953, it was clear that a second sausage-making operation, upstate from Gallipolis, was needed to meet the growing demand of supermarkets for Bob Evans sausage products. Dad, by then a father of five, did not want to leave the family in Gallipolis while he oversaw all of the details of getting the second plant up and running. It would be an all-consuming, summer-long job; plenty of late evenings and midnight oil. He wanted all of us close by. Accordingly, he found a farmhouse where he could station us while he worked. It would be an understatement to describe the place as a little rundown.

My mother recalled, "It wasn't the most pleasant experience I've had in my life.

"That house was in the middle of nowhere. I had to wash in an old wringer washer and throw the water off the back porch. Bob was working his fanny off. He had the car. The rest of us were stuck in the country: me and five children."

Though the summer exacted a considerable tribute in hard work on the part of both my parents, it was an amazing chapter–a wonderful snapshot–in the lives of our family. We came to know that particular summer in the manner we did because my father thought, in his big, sweet, but no-nonsense heart of hearts that his five offspring would gain invaluable experience and absorb amazing life lessons spending three months on a farm. With dad working day and night, we had no transportation in case of emergency or, more importantly to us, in the event of fun. One of our few outings together as a family, a trip to a drive-in movie, imprinted that season with the only name it ever needed for us children: "The summer of *Mighty Joe Young*."

Mighty Joe was an oversized ape run amuck, terrorizing the general population. Today's generation of moviegoers probably better remember a 1998 remake of the old classic I first saw in 1953. Back then, the film, a barely concealed rip-off of *King Kong*, had been making the rounds of theaters for a few summers. I don't know what kind of review dad might have given the movie. Hard as he was working, I'm sure he sneaked a nap during it. For me, it was scary, though excitingly so in the manner of ghost stories told around a campfire.

The ape saga was a cinematic analogy to a summer in which every-thing seemed possible and anything could happen. Life was good, scary, real. It was an enchanted childhood summer of visceral delights and ad-ventures. Feral and free, my brothers and sisters and I were miles from the nearest neighbor, miles from anything. But, we were young; five children aged 2 to 12. To us, everything seemed new, mystifying, fantastic and frightening–all at the same time, sometimes. My father, even back then, liked to offer his blessing on some patch of nature he had improved by liming impoverished soil or planting a stand of trees. "We've done this. Now, we'll just let nature take its course," he would say. That summer, he planted his offspring on a farm, the only place fit for growing children, and let nature take its course. And, that summer, we all shared a common awe and wonderment that can only be glimpsed from the vantage point of childhood. We didn't know then, as such knowledge is given to no one, what the future held. But for the rest of our collective lives, this particular summer would conjure up thoughts and feelings and smells of mystery in the apparent, fantasy in the familiar, and the unexplained in the recognizable. Every shadow loomed longer, every small sound in the night resonated with intrigue. There were whole worlds that existed in a rotten log or under a large stone or in a dusty hayloft. A small creek that meandered the pasture fields and skirted an old, rundown apple orchard, teemed with a universe of fascinating occupants. Tanned and tow-headed, barefoot and sinewy, we daily wore a path through waist-high wild weeds. We caught box turtles and toads, a green snake that ventured too far out from under a wood shed. All this we did in the company of a large collie we adopted and named Lady; a great, noble dog with a deep chest and long hair that was always matted with green burrs, seed pods, small sticks and hayseed. In the heat of the day, we would settle down in our secret hiding place, a small pocket in the corner of the yard beside an overgrown yew and under the generous shade of a maple. My father knew what he was doing.

It was a summer of lessons for us children, and not all of them were pleasant. We learned that if you tromp on a rusty nail, you're probably going to get a tetanus shot. Get bitten by a cat and you'll definitely get a shot. We learned that baking soda baths kill chiggers, that pigs are not cute and that a sow with babies can be downright mean.

One day, returning from blackberry picking, we decided to take a short-cut through a field of high weeds and lost a sister along the way. Aware that we could probably never convince our mother that there had actually been only four of us children to begin with, we all climbed fence posts and scanned the high weeds for the slightest hint of movement. Our collie, Lady, found 5-year-old Debbie in the same field that was to catch fire not many days later.

Our mean-tempered sow, Clementine, got out of her pen one fine July day, and I most recall of that incident how brave a figure my mother cut stalking out to the yard armed with a baseball bat, facing down that hog and shooing her back to her pen.

From the vantage point of today, I realize of that "The Summer of *Mighty Joe Young*" just how much of a beauty my dad had landed when he asked Jewell Waters to marry him. She was lovely after the manner of a dark-haired, fair-skinned, Vivian Leigh, and I still marvel at how someone so beautiful and with such dignity, could work so hard and so resiliently.

"I was stuck in the country with five young children," mother said. "The house was at the end of a dusty, remote road. Bob was working long hours, but we were young. We were healthy. We didn't have much money, but we had ambition."

At the dimming of those summer days, five Evans children commonly assembled on the back porch to fight anew the day's earlier corncob skirmish, battled from hay-bale forts in the hayloft. We were sunburned, sweat-streaked and rested contentedly beneath a veneer of dirt and dust. We ate cold, fresh watermelon and let the sweet, sticky juices dribble down our chins and along our forearms. We spit the seeds off of the back porch into the weeds. The crickets tuned up. The fireflies winked on. I don't believe my father would have been so insistent that his children get to know such a down-on-the-farm summer had there not been a room in his heart sacred to his own personal childhood memories of such seasons.

Chapter 2
Rooted in the Hills:
A Gallia County Boyhood

My birthday began with the water-
Birds, and the birds of the winged trees flying my name.
Above the farms and the white horses
And I rose
In rainy autumn
And walked abroad in a shower of all my days.

Dylan Thomas
Poem in October

The geology professors at the college I attended would have had me believe that if there was a bedrock of my father's hewing, it had to have been metamorphic, igneous or sedimentary. If they had met my dad, they would have set their science aside and agreed with my contention that the stone from which he was cut could have but one origin and history: It was Welsh. My father's lone self-indulgence of the so-called deadly sin of pride did not trade upon personal or professional success. It was rather that he had descended from a strong-hearted people with a healthy appetite for overcoming great challenge and adversity. It is, after all, a Welsh proverb that reminds us, "Adversity comes with instruction in his hand."

From the British throne, the Welsh ruled all of England from seven years before Columbus sailed to a century after he had returned. A cynic might add, "And they never forgot it either." The red dragon, *Y Draig Goch,* whose griffin-like profile graces the nation's white-over-green bicolor, is said to possess epic power over oppression and tyranny. The Welsh regard themselves as bold, resourceful, dutiful to family and proud of their heritage. It is human nature that some might view their thrift as parsimony, their pride in heritage as an insular clannishness. To the contention that the Welsh are a dark and brooding people, my father would retort that the ones who wanted to see the sun, instead of the midnight-at-noon drudgery of a life in the coal mines, came to America. And so it was that the J.L.W. Evans clan did just that.

Dad's people came in 1840. Ohio was then regarded as the West by those who occupied the more genteel reaches of the eastern seaboard. It was not until four years after my Evans forebears set foot in Ohio that the last of the native people, the Wyandot, were resettled from the state's west and north-central regions. The most likely route followed by the parents of dad's great-grandfather John L.W. Evans, was over the Alleghenies and down the Ohio River to the region of Gallia County. John was a child at the time. In 1963, when the whole of Ohio was caught up in the nation's centennial of the Civil War, my father's uncle, Robert Alton "Alt" Evans, described the odyssey of young John L.W. Evans in a monograph that remarkably foreshadowed dad's life. Alt wrote:

As I remember the story, he (J.L.W. Evans)came to this country with his parents from Wales in the year 1840, and they settled near Wales (Centerpoint), Ohio. He was six years of age then. He later got enough formal education to teach district school as a start in life. A short time later he

28

managed to buy a sawmill and went into the lumber business and, we can say, was quite successful when the rebellion was fought about the year 1862.

John married a handsome young woman named Sarah Davis, who had come from Wales to America not many years after he had arrived. By the summer of 1863, John was not only a successful farmer and orchard man, but the proprietor of both a grain mill and sawmill. By dint of sweat, perseverance and good fortune, he had amassed $5,000. The couple tended a small milking herd of roan shorthorns and several sturdy workhorses.

The couple's success survived a scary incident when, in mid-July, 1863, Confederate Gen. Robert E. Lee dispatched his cavalry Gen. Robert Hunt Morgan to inflict a raid into southern Indiana and Ohio. Lee was hoping that the diversionary tactic would compel the Union to commit troops in Ohio that he might otherwise have to face in the East following Gettysburg. Gallipolis had been a cause of worry for the Union from the outset of the war, at which time the state immediately across the Ohio River was not yet West Virginia, but Virginia. It was home to the capital of the Confederacy, at Richmond. Union troops had been posted to Gallia County at the opening of hostilities. A major supply depot for troops was established in Gallipolis, as was a hospital for wounded soldiers. Still, the allegiance of the townsfolk was not entirely with Lincoln and the Union. Several young men from the town and outlying areas "went south," as the expression goes, and signed on with the rebels.

When Morgan blazed through Raccoon Township in the summer of '63, John Evans strapped on his sword, mounted up and joined an assemblage of volunteers rushing to meet the insurgent Confederates. Uncle Alt's history suggests that while John was off to help drive Morgan out of Ohio, Sarah was trying to save the family's possessions from foraging rebels in search of fresh horses, provisions and money:

Grandma was taking care of $5,000 of their money. When old Morgan took (grandpa's) good horses out of his barn and put plugs in their place,

Grandma saw that something had to be done with this money. So, she put it in the cook stove to hide it.

Later, when the Confederates had been driven out and the terrorized citizenry had time to catch their breath, Sarah, forgetting that she had hidden the money in the cook stove, lit a fire to bake bread. Blessedly, she remembered where she had squirreled away the cache before it became the most expensive loaf she had ever baked.

When reading Uncle Alt's narrative about John, I find it difficult not to draw parallels to my father. John was continually striving to improve the bounty of his orchards by grafting and experimenting. Alt wrote of his grandfather's efforts at cattle breeding:

He was greatly interested in livestock–not only ordinary stock, but the best he could buy near or far. I well remember when he kept the milking shorthorns. At that time they were tops in the cattle breed. They were noted for the quantities of milk they gave and were also good for butter and cheese.

As did many families of that era, the Evans clan traded eggs and butter to rural peddlers for the necessities and household items they could not cultivate, raise, hatch or otherwise produce. John was an Abe Lincoln Republican whose political stripe carried on immutably all the way through to Teddy Roosevelt. He was democratic in the manner of the Great Emancipator and a steward of nature after the secular gospel Roosevelt preached on conservation. At John's funeral service at Nebo Church, two pastors, one speaking in English, the other in Welsh, invoked the message of Ecclesiastes: "A good name is better than precious ointment. The day of death is better than the day of birth for those who serve the Lord."

Had either pastor cared to turn from the 7th chapter of Ecclesiastes to the 3rd, he would have found there the words that guided the unfolding of my father's life: "To everything there is a season, and a time to every purpose under heaven."

My father's "time to be born" arrived on May 30, 1918.

In Ohio, the nation and the world, it was a time of great upheaval and uncertainty. It was also a time of infinite possibility. The world was at war the year dad was born, a war that would continue for the first six months of his life. The nation was being swept by an influenza pandemic that would claim 675,000 lives in the U.S. before it had run its course. The national life expectancy of a male born in 1918 had barely crept above 50 years. It was an era of great invention and enterprise. It was the age of Ford, Edison and Rockefeller. Dayton-born aviation pioneer Wilbur Wright, when asked several years after his historic Kitty Hawk flight to describe the ingredients necessary for a young man to find success in America, explained simply, "Pick out a good father and mother and be born in Ohio."

"A place called Sugar Ridge," dad would come to describe the patch of Ohio where he followed Wilbur Wright's advice, "in an old white house along the railroad tracks near Bowling Green." At the time my father was born, his father, Stanley, was a grocer in northwest Ohio. The family moved around as Stanley's work dictated. The grocery business was in a state of flux as the first supermarkets of fledgling chains (Kroger, A&P and Piggly Wiggly) began to supplant the nation's small independent grocers. The trickle-down consequences of this incipient trend moved Stanley, his wife Elizabeth, and their family to seek a niche where an independent could still operate and make a decent salary. Dad recalled that he attended four different schools during the first grade, and that the uprooting and relocating probably played a role in the difficulties he experienced learning to read.

The transience and tumult of early childhood ended for my father when Stanley returned to Evans family home country in Gallia County to open a grocery there in 1924. A younger Stan Evans had earned a teaching certificate from Rio Grande College at 17 and taken a teaching job in Bud, West Virginia, for the princely sum of $25 a month and a mule. An extra $5-a-month stipend was added when he agreed, additionally, to shoulder the duties of school janitor.

Now, returned to Gallipolis, Stanley began building what would eventually become a string of 16 full-service supermarkets, with in-store bakeries and meat departments, in southern Ohio, West Virginia and Kentucky. The Evanses were a self-reliant stock, Elizabeth being no exception.

"Industrious and thrifty," my mother said of the woman destined to become her mother-in-law. "Your grandmother could make a purse out of a sow's ear. She would come across worn out clothes, woolens and such, and she would gather scraps from those miserably old clothes, cut them into strips and hook them into rugs. If she'd had an education, there is no telling what she could have accomplished.

"She was a smart shopper and a wonderful cook. She was everybody's grandma.

She rocked babies and wiped noses and had a strong, contagious sense of humor. She was a fun-loving woman."

From her sprouted my father's affable and outgoing nature, along with his resourcefulness. Elizabeth took in boarders and did laundry for her husband's grocery stores. I recall her today as she prepared for Sunday services, a hat full of cherries, berries or daisies, her white tea gloves pulled on, ever-striving for an elegant appearance, though for no one so much as her God and Stanley Evans. I remember thinking of her in my childhood as the Queen of England.

To understand the imprint of dad's parents in shaping the person he became, one must know which ingredients he took from each. Both infused him with an early sense of industriousness and self-sufficiency. From his father came his business sense. From his great-hearted, generous mom, he inherited his people skills. Dad's teasing nature also came straight from Elizabeth. I can recall grandpa complaining, "Elizabeth, we need to replace a light here in the living room," and her retorting, "Well, unless they sell them at the United Methodist Church I don't know where I would pick one up since that's the only place you ever take me." It was humor, but humor with a bite.

"My mother was the thriftiest woman I've ever known," dad remembered with affection. "She taught me the value of hard work. She believed that when you made a little money you also wanted to set a little bit of it aside. Never spend your last penny."

Stanley believed that you couldn't start a child out too young to learn to make decisions. He equated decision-making with the ability to handle responsibility and, ultimately, success. Grandpa Stanley preached to my father the importance of learning the value of money. He wanted dad to know just how much a dollar was worth. To that end, he put his son to work early at his grocery—counting eggs, sweeping out the place. It was to become a lifelong belief of my father, as well as one that he advocated in abundance to his children.

That message had begun to take hold when dad was a boy delivering the *Columbus Dispatch* and selling both *The Saturday Evening Post* and the *Literary Digest*.

He remembered of his *Columbus Dispatch* paper route, "If you sold so many new customers, why, you got to go to the Ohio State Fair. I didn't even know where Columbus was, wouldn't have known how to get there. I must have been about 10 or 12 years old then. I know we stopped at Jackson at the Black Diamond restaurant. The first time I ever went to a restaurant in my life was in Jackson."

I've tried to imagine my dad as that 10-year-old boy, wide-eyed in Babylon, holding the Black Diamond's menu, smiling in sweet anticipation of his trip to the Ohio State Fair—that most wholesome, uncomplicated and quintessentially Midwestern of institutions. He was to discover that the state fair showcased a cornucopia of all things agrarian. Set cheek by jowl against the gaudy midway with its games of chance and carnival barkers, the fair was a festival of absolute superlatives: biggest, fastest, toughest, nicest, prettiest, tastiest and strangest. Perhaps it was this early experience that explained his lifelong love of that annual affair where, for years, he spent long days elbow-to-elbow with Jim Rhodes and other Ohio governors, shaking hands and meeting people, bidding at the Sale of Champions livestock auction, all the while speaking out for 4H youth, the farming community and the great State of Ohio.

Dad, on the verge of adolescence, knew he could count on two trips a year to carry him beyond the familiar confines of Gallia County. One depended upon his ability to cultivate fresh newspaper subscribers, but the other hinged simply upon his love of the Great American Pastime.

"Once a year we got to go to Cincinnati to see the Reds play," he said. "I don't think we had a radio then. We couldn't afford one. But everybody was interested in the Reds." He recalled for a reporter of his maiden trip, "The first time I went to Cincinnati, it was in a Model T. We started out at 2 o'clock in the morning and didn't get home until midnight. At the time, it was the farthest I had ever been away from home in Gallipolis."

Dad and his Gallipolis boyhood friend, Forrest Clark, also put a few coins in their pockets by chasing down chickens that had escaped from the farmers' market. The two boys often pursued the runaway fowl all the way through town and down to the banks of the Ohio River. Once captured, the chickens were placed in wooden orange crates where they were fattened until "Hayseed" (as dad was known to Forrest) and "Putzig" (as Forrest was known to dad) decided they were ready to take to market.

When dad and Putzig weren't working the angles to earn a little pocket money here or there, they were in the woods hunting. Dad remembered of those days, "Back then, you could buy a shotgun for a dollar and a box of shells for 75 cents." They knew the woods as well, if not better than, they knew the lay of the town. Putzig recalls today that he and dad used to sneak into the bell tower of the Methodist church at night carrying burlap sacks. Catching the unsuspecting pigeons perched there, they would then sell the squabs for a quarter apiece to a local restaurant. They could make a tidy sum of an evening, though Putzig said it was all too quickly squandered at the pool hall.

My father liked to joke of that era in his life, "I was so smart they voted me president of the freshman class two years in a row." It wasn't true, of course, though his liberal interpretation of attendance requirements and his tepid interest in scholastic endeavors likely did nothing to dissuade my grandfather that his only son might benefit from a change in atmosphere.

Mention the name Greenbrier to most people and it will conjure up images of the mountain splendor of West Virginia and one of the world's most elegant and storied resorts. That is not the Greenbrier from which Stanley Evans thought his son might benefit at about the time dad was preparing to start his junior year of high school. It was the other Greenbrier that caught Stanley's eye, the Lewisburg military school that billed itself as "The School of Achievement" in periodical advertisements of the day.

Established a few years before the War of 1812, Greenbrier Military School had been investing boys with a sense of discipline—both military and academic—for decades. During the Civil War, it had been pressed into service as a barracks for Union soldiers, then later as a field hospital to treat wounded combatants of both sides following the Battle of Lewisburg. It was a no-nonsense, spit-and-polish institution that boasted an ROTC affiliation with the U.S. Army. Stanley liked the prospects it offered for his son. Dad was unimpressed, at first. However, lured by the promise that he would be permitted to play football there (Gallia Academy High School had written him off, literally, as a lightweight) and that he could also take his favorite hunting dog, he relented.

"He was the only cadet in the history of Greenbrier who ever brought a dog to school," said Joe Lemon, a classmate of my father's at the school. "A lot of people had the idea that if a boy had been sent to Greenbrier it was maybe something the kid had done to deserve it. Maybe he was incorrigible. But we only had a very few of them, and Bob wasn't sent here for that. It was just a place where you could learn to respect people, study and do what you were told."

Joe Lemon's dad had left a job as a physician to miners in West Virginia's coalfields to bring his family to Lewisburg, where he opened a general practice and served as the military school's physician. Dr. Lemon held sick call at the school every morning promptly at 7:25 and, Joe said, he had good knack for unmasking cadets who were merely feigning illness to avoid drill. "He had three boys of his own."

Joe recalled that my father played baseball and football. Dad also played basketball. But, most importantly for my father, he made the school's rifle team.

Long after dad had graduated from Greenbrier, he shared a dinner at the other Greenbrier—the resort—with Joe's nephew George, an attorney and Greenbrier alum.

George remembered of that dinner, "Bob told me that coming to Greenbrier Military School was one of the greatest things that happened to him as a boy." He added with a chuckle, "Bob said that Stan thought he needed to brush up on his social skills." I wonder today how rough-edged some of those boys must have arrived at the school when I recall that the rules and regulations specified that at mealtime in the mess hall: "Knives shall not be used for carrying food to the mouth" and "spitting is considered unthinkable in gentlemen."

Cadets awakened each morning at 6:30 to the bugle blare of reveille and turned in each night at 10 to the sound of taps. For each successful day a boy completed without an infraction, he earned one merit. Merits were not disregarded as brownie points by my father. He used them to help offset his demerits. Lewisburg's Herb Pearis, both an alumnus of the school and an instructor there until the school closed in 1972, explained that something as simple as an unemptied wastebasket during room inspection could earn a cadet a demerit.

"For each demerit," Pearis said, "you had to walk around the flagpole for a half-hour. It was intended to be the most useless waste of time that anyone could imagine; a time during which you were supposed to think about how dumb you were to do whatever got you the demerits and what you could be doing if you weren't marching around a flagpole. It was supposed to make you smarter so you wouldn't do it again."

Mother said of dad at Greenbrier, "He wore his own personal path marching around the flagpole." It was never for serious breaches of regulations, though he was rumored to have been entrapped in a sting of a late-night craps game in the high reaches of the administration building's tower. Stanley mentioned the accumulation of demerits in a letter to his son, though less to upbraid than to sympathize. Stanley was too thrilled that his boy was earning As and Bs in most of his subjects to fret over demerits. He knew that dad was only adventurous and inventively ornery.

The school's newspaper, published by cadets, was often sprinkled with humorous laments about the rigors of study. One math-baffled scribe, in the year dad graduated, penned his grievance against geometry using the 23rd Psalm as a model: "Geometry is my weakness, I shall not pass," it began, running on to complain, "Surely Ds and Fs shall follow me all the days of my life." The author of that whimsy would have benefited from paying dad as a tutor, for my father, though enrolled by Stanley in a commercial course of study, was a whiz at math, particularly geometry. He was commonly summoned to the blackboard to show the balance of the class how to solve a particularly difficult problem.

For two years, my father drilled with an old hand-me-down Springfield Army rifle. He marched to his meals, never sitting to partake of them until the cadet major, armed with a sword, commanded, "Seats!" It was this type of discipline that most benefited my father's headstrong ways and single-mindedness. Dad simply learned to focus his energy and ideas, and this made his Greenbrier experience a true turning point in his life.

"He loved that school," my brother Stephen said of our father. "It was a different generation, a different time. I caught the school on its decline. Two years after I left, it closed down."

The Greenbrier Military School from which dad graduated is today the West Virginia School of Osteopathic Medicine, perhaps the only medical school in the U.S.—it has been noted—sporting a pair of gilt-painted 19th century cannons adjacent the quadrangle where dad roomed. Behind the administration building, at the far end of what is now the medical-school conference center, a museum salutes the colorful history of Greenbrier. The old school's Wall of Fame features portraits of a select four dozen of the thousands upon thousands of uniformed cadets who passed through the institution during its 164-year history. Two generals grace that wall; one who spearheaded the move to admit women cadets to the U.S. Air Force Academy, another who was assigned overall responsibility for the evacuation of Saigon in 1975 as North Vietnamese troops rolled into the capital. Some of the inductees who went on to highly decorated military careers after leaving Lewisburg, perished fighting the wars in which their battlefield bravery was saluted. A governor and two congressmen are honored on that wall. Also honored is a noted AIDS researcher whose photograph is adjacent that of a Greenbrier alum who invented the trans-dermal patch for administering medications. Below the smiling visage of one Depression-era graduate, a nameplate identifies: "Robert L. 'Bob' Evans."

Looking back over my father's life, I think the two years he spent at Greenbrier played a pivotal role in shaping him into a more focused young man. When he left for Lewisburg, he was a well of boundless energy and wild curiosity. He was a little mischievous, a bit undisciplined apropos to his "free-range" childhood. I have often said that dad, up to a point, reared himself. That point, that milestone, was Greenbrier Military School, which served to concentrate all of his diffuse energy. The sophomore at Gallia Academy High School who went away to Lewisburg was remembered by classmate Jewell Waters as a rough-edged Tom Sawyer who made his fair share of appearances in the principal's office.

Jewell was a relative newcomer to Gallia County, having relocated to the area when her father's work as a site supervisor overseeing dam construction on rivers and lakes brought the family west from its native Morgantown, North Carolina. Her roots were rural, steeped in farm life.

"My grandmother was a big, handsome, buxom woman," she says today. "She was jolly and full of humor. Ida Victoria Bickerstaff. She was a midwife, and when it was time to deliver, she would saddle up the horse and ride to the family that had called her. She stayed with them until the mother was back on her feet. She was paid for her services as a midwife in produce, in whatever the family had. She and my grandfather, Lawson Waters, had seven sons and two daughters at the foot of the Black Mountains, about 65 miles from Ashville, North Carolina.

"When my grandfather wasn't farming, he taught school. Nobody ever said anything about the Depression. My grandmother bartered with eggs to get what the family didn't produce on its own. Even then, though, there was a reading room in my grandparent's house, a bookshelf with a huge dictionary and several of what probably were considered to be the classics of American literature."

Jewell Waters was a beauty when she began her sophomore year at Gallia Academy. She recalls of the classmate she knew for only one year before he left for Greenbrier, "Your father and I weren't high school sweethearts–just friends. He was a bad boy; played hooky, went fishing.

"Once he left for Greenbrier, I didn't see him for two years. After he came home, we began to date. I had graduated from Gallia Academy in the class of 1937, but there wasn't much work for women to do back then. I was working at the dime store–G.C. Murphy & Company–in Gallipolis, selling infant wear. I worked 48 hours a week for $10.75. One day your dad came into the dime store. He had on a nice suit. We talked. He asked me what time I got off; asked if he could take me home. He started asking me for dates. We'd go to the movies, the Colony Theater in Gallipolis. You'd meet people after the show and go for sandwiches and Cokes. There was a place on the corner called the Bon Ton, kind of a youth hangout back then.

"We realized that we had a special affection for each other. It was a mutual feeling. I think the first time I actually realized that we loved each other that much--that we would one day get married--was the first year we went together. Before we dated, there had been another girl. She went off to school. When she came home from college, all of the sudden he just didn't call me anymore, and for a long time. It hurt my heart because I realized he must have had deep feelings for her, too. I thought, well, maybe he was just going with me because his girlfriend wasn't here, that he really didn't feel for me as deeply as I felt for him. So, when she went back to school, of course, he came back to see me. I told him that I thought it would be best if we didn't see each other anymore, that maybe he wanted to rekindle his relationship with his girlfriend.

"He said, 'No, no, no. I don't know what's wrong with me. I think I love you.' I knew that I loved him."

Somewhere in the distance, Bing Crosby was crooning:

It was a sudden April shower,
It was the most convenient door,
I found a million-dollar baby
In the five and ten cent store.

*Dad, age 4 1/2 with sister
Geraldine, age 2, and sister
Eva Jenny, 6. (circa 1921)*

*Dad, as a 17 year old cadet at Greenbrier
Military School. (circa 1935)*

41

Dad and mom during dad's leave from the army in 1944.

With his children Stanley, 5, and Gwen, 3, dad takes a pause on leave from the U.S. Army in 1945.

Stanley and Elizabeth Evans stand behind dad and mom and their first born, Stan.
(circa 1941)

Harold Gregor (left), dad's first employee and best friend, pause from making sausage in 1948.

Terminal Steak House, Gallipolis, Ohio, Route 7 on the Ohio River. (circa 1946)

Dad poses next to a defiant-looking Brahma bull he and his uncle Emerson purchased in Potee, Texas in 1944.

With his young, growing children in 1948. Stan, 7, right; Gwen, 5 1/2, and Robbin, 3, seated on her father's lap.

Going after a Christmas tree in 1959.

Family friend and farm hand Ilo Hurt kneels next to 2-year old Bobby.

Chapter 3

Down on the Farm:
The Homestead Life

*This is a place where grandmothers hold babies on their laps
under the stars and whisper in their ears that the lights in the sky are
holes in the floor of heaven. This is a place where the song "Jesus Loves
Me" has rocked generations to sleep, and heaven is not a concept, but
a destination.*

Rick Bragg
Somebody Told Me

Someone once said that life is what happens when we are making
other plans. At the moment when my parents realized that they were made
for one another, the "other plans" involved my father and the Ohio State
University's College of Veterinary Medicine. Dad wanted to be a vet, and
while his first two years of high school at Gallia Academy could hardly be
considered auspicious, he had managed to turn things around at Greenbrier. Even though the regimentation of life in Lewisburg failed to completely break him of his appetite for distinctly unmilitary behavior, by the time

he graduated he was posting honor-roll grades. Those grades continued when he began attending OSU, and he might well have become a doctor of veterinary medicine had he not been blind-sided by recurrent migraines.

"They were terrible," mother said. "He couldn't tolerate even the slightest bit of light in the room. Just the sound of someone walking across the floor was extremely painful." Worse, the frequency and severity of the migraines increased in proportion to the amount of time he spent poring over texts, studying for exams. His mother had suffered from the same debilitating condition in her youth. He was still in his second year at Ohio State when the attacks grew so bad that he simply had to withdraw from school.

Out of college, his professional prospects uncertain, dad took the big step he had originally intended to defer until he earned his DVM. He and mom, using a Greenbrier alumni reunion as a convenient cover, decided to elope.

"We didn't tell anybody what we were planning until just as we were pulling out," my mother said. "We told his mother and I told mine. My mother knew because she understood how much we cared for each other. His mother was very vocal: 'Don't you dare! Don't you dare!' That was her only son, and she probably had visions of something else for him. When we came home married, she cried. She was upset that your dad had brought a wife home. We stayed the first couple nights with them after the wedding. And, inevitably, we became good friends. I learned a lot from her about what I needed to know to be a wife, and I know she said kindly things about me to others. But, she was a different cup of tea. Your grandfather and I were good friends. Years after we had married, Grandpa Stanley said to me, 'The greatest decision Bob ever made was to marry you.'" Dad was to echo to me those same words when I was interviewing him for this book.

After my parents married on the first day of June, 1940, my father took a job as a salesman for the family-owned Evans Packing Company. He was on the road, going from grocery to grocery, taking orders for the family meat-packing business, though his young wife knew he had dreams of something else.

"He was a fantastic salesman," she said. "He was very good with people, but your dad, first and foremost, was always a farmer. I remember one night he came home from selling and he had a calf in the back of the car. He said, 'We can keep this calf and we can veal it, and when it is eight weeks old it will be worth this much money.' And that figure, whatever it was, was a sizable amount more than he had paid for it. Out of that came the notion that he could raise hogs and make money."

Because dad believed that a farm was the only place to rear children, he and mother took ownership of a 27-acre spread on Portsmouth Road outside of Gallipolis. It had neither indoor plumbing nor a furnace and had fallen into disrepair while waiting for someone like my father to see potential where most others would have seen only a disaster. My parents worked the place into shape as best they could. By 1944, though, the draft board that had passed over dad in the war's early going appeared to be reconsidering that decision.

"When he had to go to the Army," mother said, "we had to get rid of the house. He didn't want me out there, that far outside of town with two little babies." My brother Stan was born in 1941. By 1942, he had a baby sister, Gwen. And later, in 1945, she was pregnant with me.

My father saw plenty of enemy soldiers during his stint for Uncle Sam, though he was never in combat. As the end of the war neared, the U.S. was holding more than 425,000 German, Italian and Japanese prisoners of war. Scores of prison camps were strung out across the nation. POW facilities in the U.S. bore little resemblance to German camps holding U.S. prisoners and no resemblance at all to the conditions under which captured American servicemen suffered under Japanese control. The prisoners my father guarded had their own recreation areas and canteen. Meals were designed to assure that each POW received a minimum 2,500 calories per day. Internees were paid a token monthly stipend, permitted to take correspondence courses from any of 14 U.S. colleges, and were free to attend camp lectures on literature, art, music and history. Those who had family in the United States were allowed visitors twice a month.

Although dad was proud of his Army service, he, like many others in uniform, chafed at the regimented bureaucracy that was the central feature of military life. He had spent two years of his adolescence enduring the spit-and-polish routine at Greenbrier. When the war ended his military duty guarding captured German and Italian soldiers in Massachusetts, he was elated to return to civilian life.

Once dad had the Steak House up and running in late 1945, and the two sausage plants in full production in 1954, he caught his breath long enough to purchase the farm of which he had always dreamed. Two decades after he and mother took a mortgage on what came to be called the Homestead, my father, in a newsletter titled *Down on the Farm: Plain Talk from Bob Evans*, wrote of the place:

Its story goes back as far as Daniel Boone in the late 1700s. Even before his time, the local Indians and buffalo had made north-south trails passing right across the present farm. The farm's original settlers, Nehemiah Wood and his family, came here in 1805 from Luray, Virginia, bringing with them many former slaves. The Woods were important political leaders of the community and in their meetings at the farm they made many decisions which directed the policy and growth of the entire community. The Wood family lived in a log cabin for 20 years until they built the Homestead in 1825, using bricks fired on the farm. The building still stands. I lived there with my family for 19 years, and it has since been remodeled for use as my office and as the headquarters for farm operations.

At one time, the Homestead was a hotel, and we still have the original inn license issued in 1862. The Wood family maintained a stable and water tank for stagecoaches passing through on the way from Chillicothe (Ohio's first capital) to Gallipolis (Ohio's second oldest town) on the Ohio River.

Even though the Homestead was, for a short time, owned by Rio Grande College, only two families have ever lived there: the Wood family and the Bob Evans family.

Before there was the Homestead, to which my father affectionately alluded in *Plain Talk from Bob Evans,* we had briefly been a family of small town residents. Dad's consuming passion from the time of his earliest memory as a young boy was simply to be just a farmer "down on the farm." When he opened the Steak House the year after the war ended, it was less with an eye toward making it big in the restaurant business than simply earning enough money to buy a farm on which he could rear his children. If he knew one thing down to his marrow, it was that farm life was intrinsically good. To a city child beholding his breakfast of eggs, sausage and milk, the chicken, hog and cow from which each of those is derived is essentially an abstraction, almost a rumor. A farm child knows better. But, the road that led dad's children to their very first experience in farm living passed first through Gallipolis.

My parents built the house on Hedgewood Drive in 1948. The day we moved in, the oldest Evans child, my brother Stan, was seven. The youngest, my sister Debbie, was six weeks old. My mother, in addition to seeing to the needs of her quartet of young ones, also pinch-hit with the baking chores at the Steak House.

"I couldn't leave my children and be there," my mother said of the restaurant, "but I could bake the pies and the cakes, chop fresh vegetables for the salad." While she was busy with those tasks, my father rose each morning and traveled to the Orchard Farm, as we came to call the 300-acre place that he and his father had purchased after the Steak House opened. Harold and Marevia Cregor lived on that farm. My father, when he and Harold weren't about the business of making sausage, raised grain and cattle and put up hay.

"We'd try to wait dinner," mom recalled, "but sometimes he wouldn't get back from Orchard Farm until late. After you children went to bed, we'd stay up and visit, go over the day and our plans for the next one. We didn't have nights out. We'd take drives on Sunday afternoons, and when we did, your dad would always drive past the Homestead farm. He would say, 'This would be a great place for us. We don't want to raise our children in town. I'll see if I can buy this place. If we can raise our children on a farm, we can teach them how to be responsible.'

In 1955, the Nehemiah Wood Farm in Rio Grande became our home.

"We moved into the Homestead with five children, and everybody had a responsibility." my brother Stan recalled. "I milked two cows seven days a week. One was a Jersey. I had to put kickers on her. I also had 1,200 caged layers. We raised them up in a chicken house as pullets. I put all the cages together. One of the best lessons dad ever taught me came from those chickens. When I had eggs that were cracked, I couldn't sell them commercially. There was nothing wrong with them. They just had small cracks in them. But neighbors would come to the house and buy them. However, being a teenager and kind of lackadaisical, I sometimes wouldn't sell those cracked eggs. I didn't want to mess with them. I'd let them get too old to sell. One day dad sat down with me and said, 'I'm going to tell you something, Stan. You remember this. The good eggs you sell pay for the chickens and their feed. They pay for all the expenses, and on top of that you make a little profit, too. But the cracked eggs are all pure profit because all of your expenses have already been paid for with the good eggs. So, every time you don't sell a cracked egg you are losing pure profit.'"

Dad understood from his own childhood and youth that responsibility had to be entwined with rewards if lessons on the importance of self-reliance, initiative and resourcefulness were going to take. Stan kept $10 a week out of his egg profits for spending money. And, at the same time he was learning to make his own way, he was also employing my sister Gwen and me as sub-contractors in his operations. While he was candling the eggs, we would help out with the packaging. In return for that assistance,

I was allowed to adopt the hens that weren't laying regularly. I kept them separate from his regular layers, and when they would produce a dozen or so eggs, those would be mine to take to Rio Grande and Denny's general store and Frank Denny would buy them from me.

It was dad's "full circle" principle pure and simple.

"I got paid for milking the cows," Stan explained, "by getting their calves each year. I would raise the calves up to 200 pounds, then sell them at the stockyards. I started raising sheep at 14 or 15. When lambing came around, I built a room in the hayloft out of bales of hay. I put a sleeping bag up there and an alarm clock, and I would sleep in the barn. It was February and colder than hell. I'd set the alarm, and every hour and a half I would go down and check the sheep."

"All of you children belonged to 4H," mother remembered, "and that was a wonderful part of your lives. You all loved being here at the Home-stead. You kids never wanted to go to the city. I think that when we moved there, you all were enamored of the notion that you were going to live on a farm, that you would get to see this and that, but I don't think any of you children loved the farm as much as your dad. You guys didn't realize how much hard work was involved. Your dad liked the farm for the reasons that people have farms. He liked to see what it could produce, what the land could do for you. And he wanted to make sure that you children appreci-ated those same qualities about the place."

The Homestead was a laboratory in which my father was continually experimenting with the earth and with the livestock, while at the same time making those experiments an exercise in parenting that would infuse us children with a sense of self-worth. It was never imparted in a man-ner that indicated he thought of himself as an all-wise agrarian. I think he realized that he was merely a crucible that transported a vital cargo of life lessons to his offspring. After all, as a child, he was given a wide berth. He was given enough space and time to learn things for himself, explore life, respect the value of work and cultivate a capacity for awe about nature and its workings. He understood that nature possessed all manner of arrestingly engaging wonders. He also knew that the same nature that held the power to amaze and delight his children, could also break their hearts when it took as readily as it gave.

My older sister Gwen raised prize steers, and I remember that one year, just before she was about to show one at the fair, she came screaming to my brother Stan that something terrible was wrong with one of them. At the time, Stan was candling eggs. He set aside his work and rushed to find Gwen's best hope for a county-fair blue ribbon lying on his side in the barn. She had spent nine months raising that steer. Not only was it a cinch to win champion steer, but she loved it dearly, as well. It was like a big fat baby to her. Her steer had shown a tendency toward bloating. Had it been only a minor instance of the problem, it would have been possible to summon a vet who might pass a tube to relieve the condition. But the steer lay near death. Stan had only one choice left to him.

"You put your hands on the side of the steer," he said, "and you measure: so far from that bone. And that is where you stick the knife."

And, as Gwen watched anguished, he did.

"But it was too late," Stan said.

Now that I look back on that incident, sad as it was, I cannot help but understand with the acute clarity retrospect lends to remembered crisis just how much nature was a teacher to all of us. Growing up on the Homestead, I know now that there were certain lessons only my father could have taught us and just as many that were the sole dominion of my mother. The balance, only nature could reveal.

My mother possesses a treasure of mental snapshots from that era to remind her of the days when we children were being schooled unaware about life on the farm.

"They've just come home from school," she recalled of a day at the Homestead. "You, Robbin, have your little portable radio under your arm and you are on your way down to the barn. You're carrying a pail. You've got to wash the cows' udders before you milk, but you have music while you're working. We have an intercom between the kitchen and the barn. I'd turn it on and hear the craziest music in the world, and the kids would be laughing and having fun. Maybe somebody had come home from school with them. Then, before long, on the intercom, I'd hear, 'Mom, what's for supper?'

"Your father was gone a lot then, but you guys knew what had to be done. Sometimes I had to nudge you all a little. Let's say it was Steve. It would be evening and spitting snow. It's cold. I'd say, 'Steve, have you fed your sheep? Have you checked their water to see that it's not frozen?' And he hadn't. I'd tell him, 'That is your responsibility, and you can't go to bed until you've taken care of it.'"

It would be utterly impossible to tell any story at all about the Homestead Farm and the 17 years we all spent there without including two important people whose lives were inextricably linked with ours by the nature of the fact that we shared them daily with each other: a young married couple, Lucy and Ilo Hurt. They were an extension of our family.

Unbeknownst to us, their family had been kinsmen with ours for more than three generations, by the time on that gray, February day, Lucy knocked on the side door to the kitchen of our home. Mother answered the door and Lucy beamed her wonderful smile, inquiring as she did, "Missus Evans, do you need someone to help you in this big house?"

It was instantaneous success. It was serendipity of the highest order. Lucy not only helped run the house, cleaned, cooked, wiped noses and tears; she Band-Aided skinned knees, fixed doll babies, rocked away hurt feelings; and, found lost dump trucks under beds. When working alone in the house, she was also known to sing in a beautiful low soprano voice. She sang hymns, Sinatra, Crosby, classics, just any tune that struck her fancy and many of which she made up. Lucy was always cheerful; always with a smile and a helpful attitude. She would do anything asked of her short of reprimands and spankings.

Lucy was tall and stately, very attractive in a handsome way. She was well-read. She wore her hair pinned up into a bun that circled the bottom of her head. It was a popular style of the day. We children thought she looked like an angel.

The best way to describe Ilo is that he was very tall and skinny and had the profile of a scarecrow. I never saw Ilo with his hat off—not once in 17 years. Ilo worked on the farm as a hand and around the house for mother. He was a jack of all trades. He could fix anything and he did. He was somehow always within earshot of mother if she needed him, unless there were some big doings on the farm that day—putting up silage, fixing fences, mowing, at which time he worked with the other men on the farm. Each morning, just at dawn, Ilo would come into the big family room of the Homestead and build a huge fire in the fireplace. By the time we children came downstairs for breakfast, it would be ablaze, casting real warmth (the much better kind, the cozy kind) all around the big room. Ilo would crouch down on the rug by the kitchen door and visit with us children as we ate our breakfast, which Lucy was usually preparing at the time. Ilo genuinely liked children, and he loved to talk to us every morning. He was always smiling, too. We all loved Ilo.

I remember when my little brother Bobby was just a tot. I was 13 when he was born; he was the last of six. Bobby followed Ilo around all day. He stood in Ilo's shadow from dawn 'til dusk, learning such things as: how to call a milk cow into the barn; the best place to find good fishing worms for bait; how to set a perfect trap for barn rats; how to roll your own smokes; how to tell what the weather is going to do six to eight hours before it is going to do it; the best way to skin a squirrel; how you can tell when a sow is about to whelp, and the list goes on *ad inifinitum*. Presently, Bobby is a very successful real estate broker in Bozeman, Montana. I have wondered through the years, just how Bob has been able to call all of this education into play in his chosen profession. And, I am dead sure, without a shadow of a doubt, that everything he learned from Ilo has helped him immeasurably in his life. Just having the privilege of knowing Ilo did a great deal for me. Ilo taught me how to milk our cow, Cordelia, when I was 13. He passed away many years ago now, but at the time of this printing, we still have our Lucy and we are grateful for that.

Those days at the Homestead with Ilo and Lucy were the days when dad was trying to grow the sausage business. It was a tiresome and time-consuming process, because each city targeted as a new market had to be tackled one supermarket or grocery at a time. And, at that early stage, much of the shoe leather being worn out was his.

"They called it opening up a town," Stan said of dad's forays into new market areas. "He would go into the newspaper office and get a list of every grocery store in town that advertised in the paper. Then he and whoever might be with him would divide those stores into sections and go call on those customers. Dad might be opening up Toledo, say, and he would work at it all day then he would drive home that night so he could be with us, his family. It meant he had to get up the next morning to drive all the way back up to Toledo to go at it again."

Dad wanted to be part of everything that happened at the Homestead. Still, at the same time, he knew that if the sausage business was going to succeed, his work days might commonly have him as far away as Cleveland or Youngstown. He might be several days in those cities, but I can't recall a day he didn't deadhead it back home from Cuyahoga or Mahoning County to make sure he slept at night under the same roof with mom and all of us.

For as much as my father loved his children, each of us wanted to be loved back by him in a way that wasn't collective. Each of us wanted to be individually appreciated by him; be recognized for something that made dad proud. For Stan, the oldest, that meant setting the example for the rest of us through his industriousness and youthful ability to, essentially, run his own small and various operations. That included the milking, raising sheep and looking after the 1,200 laying hens that comprised his egg business. Gwen made my father proud by raising steers, but she also won his heart by charm. She was an enchantress who could turn dad to butter in her hands just by throwing her arms around his neck and giving him a hug. I don't know why or how I knew that the way to my father's heart was through horses.

I suppose my dad fell in love with horses as a child, and probably because, at the the most tender of ages, his family was either too poor or too often moving from place to place for him to have one. It meant enough to him that, even when we were living in the small town of Gallipolis in what could only be called a tract subdivision, we had a pony in a field below our house. Her name was Candy. She was brown and white. And, she could be a spiteful little beast. She would nip at you if you got close enough and sometimes kick. Dad wouldn't let anyone ride her unless he was close at hand, but I suppose that despite her ill-tempered nature, she was the reason I fell in love with horses. Also, it didn't take much precocity to see that dad looked at horses in a different way than he viewed the wide array of animals that comprise a working farm. Hogs intrigued him because they were vital to his business. He had a great love of cattle, particularly Charolais. Sheep and chickens could be moneymakers on a working farm. But all of those had to be viewed as cash-crop propositions, and he knew the central truth of the old saw, "Wherever you have livestock you're going to have dead stock." That was simply part of life on the farm. Horses, though, were something else to him. Of all the photographs ever taken of dad when he was "down on the farm," few engage me as much as those that captured him on horseback.

I recall a Christmas my father bought me a Palomino. I should have known that something was up a week before the 25th when Gwen and Debbie began giving me the cold shoulder.

"Robbin, I want you to come out to the front porch," dad said as the family was all gathered around the tree. I was about 12 at the time and, truth be told, that Palomino mare gave me plenty of reasons not to like horses. She threw me not long after I began riding her. I was on the ground, and tried to grab the reins, but, as I did, she wheeled around and kicked me in the backside with a stunning wallop. I ended up not only with a perfect horseshoe bruise on my rump, but also with a bad case of whiplash. It wouldn't be the last time a horse threw me. I had a Tennessee Walking Horse that ran along the fence line using the overhanging branches and tree limbs to try to scrape me off. At 16, I climbed on a mare unaware that she was being tormented by a subcutaneous boil that was merely aggravated when I cinched her up. She threw me off and, when I hit the dew-covered grass, I slid under a wooden fence. I checked myself. Nothing was broken. I'm fine, I thought until I looked down to see that my right spur was imbedded in my left leg.

"I'm going to kill that horse," dad blustered. He didn't, of course. It was merely his protective, paternal side coming out. As close as he came to fulfilling such an oath, though, was the day—ironically it happened to be Father's Day—when I was attacked by a big Quarter-Horse stud after dad had asked me to round up a pair of mounts for a trail ride he was planning for the next day. I had reined a couple of geldings when I heard the ominous thud of hoof beats behind me and turned around to see the stud, who had just leaped a cattle guard, bearing down on me. It might have been a rush of equine testosterone that spurred the attack, for I was not far from the pasture where his mares were grazing. I attempted to turn so as to use the pair of horses I was leading as a buffer, but he sank those big horse teeth directly into the top of my thigh, not once, but twice. Dad did his best to intervene, hurling dirt clods at my attacker.

I was rushed to the hospital. As my jeans were being scissored off, my father tried to console me.

The attending physician didn't help matters when he marveled, "I think the only worse bite I've ever seen was when a hog chewed off the back of a boy's leg."

When I look back now on all of the scrapes and bruises, bites and scars that were small reminders of growing up on a working farm, there is nothing about it for which I would have traded places with a princess. If the 1950s and early '60s were a fascinating time to be growing up in America, doing so on a farm made it an even more incredibly broadening experience for my siblings and me. Gallipolis was close enough that whenever we wanted a dose of town life, it was both within easy reach and yet sufficiently small that my father didn't worry about big-city threats or temptations. Barely a city—5,000 residents being a requisite of such status in Ohio—Gallipolis was a place for us to walk and gawk and watch the barges shoving tow on the river.

We were bona fide rubes, and I was the biggest yokel of all. We just strolled up and down the street to see who we could see. There was a jewelry store that sold 45 rpm records in the back, and dad's drive-in restaurant was always a draw. It was, in the late '50s, a genuine Midwestern microcosm of *American Graffiti.* Sooner or later, most every local teenager with a driver's license and a set of wheels took his place in the polished-chrome promenade that circled the curb-service stalls at the drive-in where nothing much more than French fries and Cokes were ever ordered. I could watch it all play out from my father's Steak House next door, where I waited tables for 75 cents an hour plus tips. It didn't take much to make a girl homesick for the Homestead in 1961, though, by the time I was in high school, in 1962, it was becoming clear that the sanctuary the farm had always been was becoming hostage to the popularity of the Bob Evans name.

Dad was doing his own TV commercials for sausage, and when the advertising firm's film crew arrived at the Homestead from Columbus, nothing on two legs or four was safe from being conscripted into the production. The earliest TV ads simply depicted dad in a studio chatting up his product to an invisible audience. He was straightforward and plain-spoken, an endearing hint of Appalachian twang in his voice. He knew that the founding tenet of advertising dictated that the sizzle be sold along with the steak. He wasn't a man simply promoting sausage. "Made by a farmer on the farm," he would tell the rolling camera. That, pure and undiluted, was my father. He was a farmer, and he made his sausage on the farm. Dad would tell us that he had an unfair advantage over others who also stood astride businesses they had grown from scratch: His company didn't have to make him up. He was not some iconic, Betty Crocker marketing tool, hand-crafted and smoothed in order to be trotted before the consuming public. He was selling down-on-the-farm wholesomeness, and it hit a respondent chord not only with viewers who had once lived on a farm, but also, and perhaps more particularly, with city folks who wished they had.

"Folks," he would assure viewers of his TV commercials, "if this is not the best sausage you've ever eaten we'll give you your money back." He said it with an honest country twang and a broad engaging smile. "It's best by a country mile."

It didn't take long for dad to work both his family and the inviting environment of the Homestead into the TV ads. Today, some of those old black and white commercials seem positively hilarious. One of my favorites depicts a party of teenagers dancing the twist as they work up an appetite for Bob Evans sausage sandwiches. A teen band is rocking down in the background as the hostess enters from stage left with a pyramid of sausage sandwiches atop a large platter. I'm sure that teen heart throb Frankie Avalon never whispered to Annette Funicello, "Boy, making out on the beach sure is fun, but I could really go for a Bob Evans sausage sandwich." Still, we had a lot of fun on the advertising set during the process of the elaborate productions. It made for great memories.

The teen twist party commercial was shot in a studio, though many of TV spots were filmed at home. While those productions staged at the Homestead were novel and intriguing events, they also foreshadowed a coming change for my father and our family. The shoots for television commercials were often protracted, wearying events during which the whole house was thrown into a state of disarray. With the advertising crew underfoot, with production assistants running here and there arranging all of us at the kitchen table or out on the patio, the place we called home ceased for a while being our family sanctuary. Our privacy was becoming an occasional hostage to success. The growth of my father's business moved apace the growth of his children. When I was three years old, in 1948, Bob Evans Sausage was nothing more than dad and Harold Cregor diving into a business founded on $500 of my father's money and $500 from his father, Stanley. It was two men with three hogs, 50 pounds of sage, 40 pounds of black pepper and an idea. By my fifth birthday, the business had its very own pole barn, one fulltime and a few part-time employees. By the time I was 8, the company had incorporated as Bob Evans Farms. In 1957, the year I reached 12, almost 2,000 groceries and supermarkets were selling the sausage that bore dad's name.

Befitting my father's big-hearted, affable manner, his television ads selling all of that sausage often closed with him inviting a vast unseen TV audience, "Come on down and visit us." And they did. My mother would start out the back door to hang the wash or shake the rugs only to discover strangers armed with cameras peeking about the premises. Dad also would commonly invite business associates down to the Homestead for a trail ride. It fell to me to help entertain these slickers by saddling them up and heading for the hills.

I understood completely why dad's urban guests found the Homestead engaging. I had fallen in love with it from the start. From my bedroom window, when the maples were winter bare, I could look out across the valley all the way to Granny's branch and the adjacent pond. The hills of Gallia County in that part of my home country are bunched together like throw pillows of cool greens and loden set against the headboard of the horizon. They are beautiful any time of year, but the first sign of spring was always a special time for me. The lambing was finished, mares were foaling, cows calving. The continuum of nature and life could be glimpsed firsthand. Most memorable though, in all of this harkening, was the scent of the earth after the thaw—a pleasant aromatic fecundity. Autumn possessed the capacity to fill me with a wistful melancholy with its showering of saffron, sorrel and crimson leaves signaling a turning inward of life as we battened down the hatches for winter. Spring, though, with everything around the Homestead unfolding outward, brought only exuberance.

As a way of buffering this incredible treasure from curiosity seekers while still making good on dad's invitation to satisfied customers to "come on down" to Rio Grande, my father decided, in 1961, to open what came to be known as the Sausage Shop. In its initial incarnation, it was even smaller than the original Steak House. Located hard by the edge of Rt. 35 just down the hill from the Homestead, it sported four stools and six small tables where drop ins could grab a quick bite of Bob Evans famous product without driving all the way to Gallipolis, a dozen miles distant. The place was painted red, a bellwether hue for things to come. The first menu was a model of culinary minimalism, its staple being the sausage sandwich. As traditional with any of dad's ventures, my mother kitchen-tested the bill of fare before the doors opened on the first day.

The Sausage Shop was an instant success and, looking back on it, its opening marked the beginning of Bob Evans going public. Two years would pass after the place served its first customers before Bob Evans Farms, Inc. went public, but the first intimations were clear that what had begun as a private dwelling was becoming a public destination.

I was home from college, writing a letter to a friend one day, when I looked up from my correspondence at the kitchen table only to glimpse a small knot of people looking back at me. Time has robbed me of the particulars of that assemblage. It might have been a group dad had invited down or merely a handful of Sausage Shop customers checking out the place while digesting lunch. It is important less for the details than the significance for, somehow in that moment, I knew that while a part of my father's life would always be personal and much-cherished treasure to me, much of it would belong to the public, to the people whose favor helped fashion his success.

Chapter 4
"How to Win Friends and Influence People"

There are some people who have the quality of richness and joy in them, and they communicate it to everything they touch. It is first of all a physical quality; then it is a quality of the spirit.

Thomas Wolfe

My father tithed at Simpson Chapel, but inasmuch as he believed in God, he believed every bit as much in people. The evolution of this curious theology perplexed me in my youth. Mother would roust us all early Sunday morning, make sure that we were all scrubbed, combed and polished, then march us out the door to church. Sometimes my father would join this procession of Christian soldiers "marching as to war." Other times, I would catch a glimpse of him as we exited. As often as not, he would be clad in a worn flannel shirt, poring over a copy of the *Farm Journal* as he listened to the sonorous strains of Tennessee Ernie Ford caressing *Old Rugged Cross* or *Amazing Grace*. On many a Sabbath, that was church for my father.

Dad was a Golden Rule egalitarian, a disciple of the notion that everyone who passed his way in life was as forthright and honest as he was. Some would prove themselves unworthy of such trust, but, in large measure, the actions of those who became partners in his life's successes simply confirmed what he believed about the inherent goodness of humankind. Over time, I came to understand that while the earth and all that it produced and sustained was the mother church of my father's spiritual ideology, people represented its enduring articles of faith. In his own peculiar way, dad was an unwavering proselytizer of people. He didn't knock on their doors and ask them if they knew where they would spend eternity, but he could be tenaciously persistent in enticing them to come take a seat beneath the spread canvas revival tent of his vision for the future. When he was first starting out in business, he tracked down his friend Harold Cregor all the way to a steel mill in Youngstown.

"He'd find out where you were if he liked you," Harold said. "He called me up in Youngstown and said, 'I need you. I got a job for you back here.'"

Dad knew that Harold and Marevia, a young, hard-working couple from Kentucky, had gone off seeking a better life in a smoke-belching Gomorrah full of strangers, and couldn't possibly be happy there. He persuaded the two to move back to Gallia County and oversee the property that he and his father had purchased and named Orchard Farm. More than running the farm, though, Harold was a jack of all trades trusted implicitly by my father to handle any task that needed to be done from the Steak House to the sausage-making operation to the farming. Plain and simple, dad believed in Harold in the manner that a beginning seminarian believes in the statues to which he prays.

Dad was the same way with Elmer Hill, who joined the business at a time when my father needed the fingers of only one hand to count his employees.

"I had played some baseball with Bob," Elmer recalled recently of their first connection with one another in Gallipolis. The two had lost touch after they married and began raising their families.

"I was working at the brickyards in Oak Hill," Elmer said. "I came home from work one day and your dad was waiting on me in the yard. 'You've got some awfully nice kids here, Elmer,' he said. We talked some. He told me, 'I want you to come to work for me.' I said, 'Bob, I'm making pretty good money.' He said, 'But it's a dangerous job.' He was right. I knew it. Several people who worked there didn't live too long after they left.

"Your dad said, 'Elmer, I can only pay you $1.05 an hour.' I told him, 'I can't make it with all these kids on that kind of money.' He said, 'I know you're a worker. I'll tell you what I'll do. I'll start you out at $1.25 an hour and give you a raise every 90 days until you're making what you need for your family.' He kept his word. You could depend on what your dad told you.

"I'd be working at the plant, and Jewell would call me. She knew I had a houseful of kids. Your dad and mom had a few cows. She'd give me butter, milk. I never had anybody help me with my family like that. They did us right. If I needed a little loan, it was there. I owned shares in the company.

"I got the calling while I was working for your dad. I was ordained in 1964 in the Free Will Baptist Church. If I had to do a funeral on a work day, your dad would let me go and pay me for the time I was gone. He had to have faith in God to live the life he did. I know that he honored God."

He did, but my father's way of showing it was to honor people. He knew that a rising tide lifts all boats and that those who had invested their time, elbow grease and sweat in his dream would benefit in abundance for their faith.

I once heard a story that reminds me to this day of dad's beliefs. It seems that a small farm went on the market one December and a fellow who had been searching for a little spread where he could work the furrows and tend the land put in a bid for it. The bid wasn't much, but then neither was the farm. The fields hadn't been cultivated in a while and were weed-strewn and overgrown. The fences required mending. The farmhouse needed a paint job. Vandals had knocked out a few of its windows. The barn and a few of the out buildings were looking a little down at the heels. But, when the bid was accepted, the fellow was ecstatic. He spent a good part of the winter bush-hogging, clearing the fields and repairing fence. He started plowing on the cusp of spring. When it was too wet to work the fields, he pitched himself at the business of putting the house in order. The broken windows were replaced and, until he lost light at day's end, he scraped old and flaking paint to prepare the house for a new coat. He fertilized and planted, even put in a flower garden along the front porch. By early July, the corn was coming on strong, the front of the house glistened beneath a fresh coat of paint and the fellow was eagerly looking forward to his first harvest. It so happened that one morning, as the young farmer strolled down the lane to fetch the mail a new pastor from a church in town was making his way along the road, stopping at farms to invite folks to come worship on Sunday. He reached the dramatically restored farm at about the same time the farmer reached his mailbox. Drinking in the green vista, the minister, seeing his chance to present a reminder of the source of all blessings, marveled, "My, you and the Lord certainly run a fine-looking farm." The farmer sized up the clergyman but a moment before replying, "Yes, we do. But you should have seen it when the Lord was running it by himself."

Dad knew that having vision without well chosen people was like faith without works.

Sometimes, the people who teamed up with him in the pioneering years of his business came to him by pure serendipity. When he was fresh out of the Army and just getting the Steak House off the ground, in 1945, another young veteran who would prove instrumental in the success of Bob Evans Farms was working right under his nose on Eastern Avenue.

"When I came out of the Marine Corps," Bob Wood remembered of his post-war job search, "I was hired as a bookkeeper for the truck terminal there. I ran the parts department, sold bottled gas. Your dad and Herb Bush had just opened up the Steak House. I was right across the driveway." He left the terminal job in 1949 to help run a general store and mill. Uncle Sam called on him again during the Korean War and my Uncle Emerson Evans dialed his number after his second tour of duty with the Marines.

Bob recalled of the exchange with dad's uncle, the chief bean counter for the sausage business, "Emerson said, 'Wood, I want to talk to you. We've got a little business over in Xenia making sausage. I don't know if it is going to go belly up or not, but if you take the job and it does go belly up, we'll move you back here.'"

My great-uncle Emerson was the consummate financial advisor of company operations. His pencils were always sharpened and his number-crunching kept him up nights. Because he was a banker, by profession, he was a good fit for job of reckoning the ledgers. Wood was fond of recounting the story of how, when wildly fluctuating hog prices placed the sausage business in a precarious financial position, Uncle Emerson deliberately sent the wrong checks to suppliers in order to buy a few days time to stabilize matters. Emerson Evans was, someone said, a "cut-to-the-chase" guy who always had one eye trained on the bottom line. It would have been difficult to find a man who was more the polar opposite to my father. While dad was too much of a visionary and entrepreneur to think about failure, Emerson's job was to remind everyone in the room that a weather forecast predicting an 80 percent chance of sun actually was intended to warn the public of a 20 percent chance of clouds, perhaps rain, maybe even a tornado.

Richard "Mac" McLaren, a premier salesman for Bob Evans Farms from the 1960s to the 1990s, said that Emerson demanded a 14-day turnaround on money owed by groceries and required Mac and all the other route salesman to check out to the penny at the close of each day.

"He didn't talk a lot to you," Mac said of Emerson, contrasting of dad, "Your dad was soft-spoken, easy-going in the stores. He did the relationships, and he knew exactly what was going on."

Dad would have known the nature of his salesmen's relationships with the customers, because he had been out on the road selling his product for years by then. Stopping at a grocery, he'd introduce himself to the proprietor, talk a little Reds baseball maybe, then hand the man a pound of sausage and invite, "I want you to take this home and you and your wife try it. See what you think. I believe you'll like it. I'll be coming back this way in a week." He possessed an intuitive grasp of what it took to sell primarily because he recognized that beneath all of it, it was as much about a human connection—the initiation of a relationship--as it was about sausage and money.

My father knew that as long as he had salesmen such as Mac running the routes, sales operations would run smoothly with good customer relations in excellent order. Again, it was my dad's unswerving faith in people that got the job done. Day after day, Mac would be out on the road in a 1956 Chevrolet milk truck filled with sausage for the Columbus east side route. He was affable after the manner of dad and instinctively knew how to tailor his pitch to the prospect. In 35 years with Bob Evans Farms, Mac went through 27 vehicles and logged 3.2 million miles.

As with many people who came to work for my father, Mac contends that there was something in the nature of dad that made you want to do well for him. "He knew I was performing," Mac said of the numbers he was producing, "because your dad was a salesman, too. He sold himself every day, every minute his eyes were open he was a salesman."

It is not widely known, but one of the things that made dad a good salesman was a book, first published in 1937, titled *How to Win Friends and Influence People.* It was authored by Dale Carnegie, a self-taught expert in the field of self-improvement and interpersonal skills. The gospel according to Carnegie advised its disciples to repeat again and again to themselves—almost as a sort of chant—"My popularity, my happiness and sense of worth depend to no small extent upon my skill in dealing with people." Carnegie believed that the laws of human nature assured that the vast range of people who passed through our lives would include more than a few who were cold or intractable, unsociable or resistant, bull-headed or suspicious of everyone around them. Carnegie believed, assuming that we did not possess those difficult traits ourselves, that there resided within each of us the power to alter other peoples' behavior by altering how we reacted to them. He argued that one of the strongest and most enduring human needs was the desire to feel important, and that it was possible to disarm negative traits in others my making them understand that they were genuinely appreciated for the job they were carrying out. Carnegie was careful to articulate the important distinction between appreciation and flattery, for while the latter employed only words, the former required heart. Carnegie had learned much about the human desire for a defined sense of self-worth while growing up on a farm in Missouri. He had milked cows, raised hogs, sold lard, bacon and soap. His ideas about handling human transactions came early in life.

Similarly, my father's experience as a youth had prepared him in diverse and eclectic ways to view his world as an artist's palette of opportunity. He had outgrown the fear of failure at a very early age when he and his buddy, Putzig, were delivering newspapers, hawking magazines, raising rabbits, selling chickens and catching pigeons in the belfry of the Methodist Church. He always said of those days, "I had the privilege of being poor." It was not an economic situation that he lorded over his children, rather a personal circumstance of childhood that he respected for the incentive and inventiveness it gave him to make his own way. He was raised without a safety net. His father was working most of the time and rarely home. Many of the traits that define Bob Evans the man, were cultivated by my grandmother. Though uneducated in the traditional sense of the word, she was spirited, strong, self-possessed, energetic and completely fearless. The adage, "The apple doesn't fall far from the tree," comes immediately to mind. Being poor taught dad to take advantage of every opportunity that came his way. He was cunning and street smart, and he could smell an advantage, an edge, an opportunity, a mile away. He was somehow blessed with the great gift of knowing precisely the right thing to do at exactly the right time. It didn't hurt that he happened to be born to an era in this country when a man could accomplish great things by sheer force of personal will propelling a dream. To borrow an expression, some men see things as they are and ask, "Why?" My father dreamed things not yet a reality and asked, "Why not?" Being both impervious and indifferent to praise or blame, he possessed a boundless optimism that laughed in the face of conventions such as "downside planning" or any type of negativism in the boardroom. Though not authoritarian, he possessed a natural authority. Coupled with an extraordinary energy, it produced a bedrock foundation for a company that notched the hard-won admiration of both his contemporaries and his competitors.

"Your dad's right-hand people were the true salt of the earth," Bob Wood said of my father and those who came to work for him, "and he cared about those kind of people more than most people did." My father understood that natives of Appalachia are sometimes sold short by more urbane and cosmopolitan city folks. During the 1940s and '50s, Ohio, along with other Midwestern states witnessed a tremendous in-road migration into the cities from hills and hollows. These people pressed into places such as Columbus, taking jobs at the plants of Curtiss-Wright, General Motors, Westinghouse and Western Electric. Dad counted on them, these people from the heart of his home country as a treasure and a blessing. They worked in the sausage plants, ran the truck routes. So many doors were opened to them that Bob Wood said of the joke around the company, "If you wanted to be in management at Bob Evans, you had to have been born south of U.S. 40."

By the time the 1960s arrived, the business dad had launched in Appalachia was changing the way the nation viewed a product consumers had once looked down upon. This success had been etched despite the consistent problem that the chief ingredient was prone to dramatic fluctuations in price as the hog market moved through cycles which, while predictable to a certain degree, were no less unsettling. When the price of hogs was up, farmers were enticed to raise them, which drove the price down. When the price bottomed out, farmers turned to other pursuits, which caused the price of hogs to skyrocket. Dad realized that he needed to diversify the company if it was going to survive, much less thrive.

Bob Wood said, "There wouldn't be a Bob Evans Farms today if he hadn't put the concept of sausage and restaurants together."

When my father first started out in business, in 1945, the Steak House was the chief marketing outlet for the sausage he was making. But, as the sausage business took hold in supermarkets and groceries, and as Bob Evans sausage in particular changed and broadened the demographic of the product dramatically, sales for home dinner tables dwarfed the significance of the restaurant side of operations. I'm not sure exactly when it dawned on dad that growing the restaurant side of his company would provide a natural hedge against roller-coaster costs on the supermarket end of the business. It was a stroke of genius that came at a time when the dining habits of the nation were changing in stunning and remarkable ways.

In 1946, when the Steak House opened its doors, Americans were spending slightly more than 25 cents of each food dollar dining out. Considering the fact that, in 2008, that percentage is almost 50 cents on a dollar, it is easy to see why a number of revolutionary changes accompanied a 100-percent growth in what Americans spent on food prepared outside the home.

Ironically, when dad decided to grow the restaurant business, he already had a franchising icon within the Bob Evans Steak House, in Gallipolis. My father had met Colonel Harlan Sanders at a food show in the

1950s. Sanders, of Corbin, Kentucky, had been distinguished as a colonel by Kentucky's Depression-era Governor Ruby Laffoon, and he played the honorary distinction for all it was worth. Although Sanders didn't get into the franchising game until he was 65, no one pursued it with more vigor, zest and color. He cultivated a persona around his white suit, cane, string tie, snowy mane and goatee. It must have worked, for while the Colonel is many years gone, his caricatured visage remains part of KFC. He was, dad always contended, quite a showman, bigger than life, and a good man.

Sanders might have been content to spend his golden years running the Harlan Sanders Café in Corbin had not the coming of the interstate threatened its extinction. With I-75 set to pass him by, he began selling franchises to his "secret recipe" chicken wherever he could. When Kentucky Fried Chicken became part of the bill of fare at the Bob Evans Steak House, the deal was cinched with a handshake. Not only did the agreement sell a lot of chicken in Gallipolis, it also provided dad with a smorgasbord of food for thought.

The school of human nature had no more ardent a scholar than my father. He would study men such as the Colonel to learn what motivated them, why their ideas worked and what they had to teach. He would file away those lessons for the time when he would need them, and as the 1960s began drawing to a close, he knew that time was at hand.

Any entrepreneur studying the restaurant landscape in America in 1967 could see clearly that the trend was moving swiftly toward fast food operations. In 1961, Ray Kroc had bought out a pair of West Coast brothers named McDonald and launched their golden arches and no-frills approach into the stratosphere. Burger King was taking off in Florida, and Hardees out of North Carolina. Closer to home in Columbus, while the drive-in fad had been saturated by Big Boy, Big Bev, Jerry's and Green Gables, fast food operations were relatively scarce. Like all trends and fashions, everything moves from the West Coast east. More circumspect Midwesterners have to look over a novel item to make sure it doesn't bite.

One of the first to arrive on fast food scene in Columbus was an entrepreneur named Roy Tuggle. His brainchild was Burger Boy Food-o-Rama. Similar to the concept established by the McDonald brothers in California, it was lean on amenities and fast on service. Where, in the past, even the most bare bones of luncheonettes had served a burger and French fries on a non-disposable plate, Burger Boys were wrapped in paper and served in sacks. The operation required neither car hops outside nor waitresses inside. It was hugely popular with young diners and arrived on the scene just as first-cusp baby boomers with discretionary income were getting their drivers licenses. Dad, ever a student of ergonomics, liked the way Burger Boys had been designed so that food preparation required the fewest steps and the least wasted motion.

Intrigued by what he could learn from studying success, dad signed on as a grill cook at a Burger Boy. By this time, in 1965, he and Tuggle had become friends. My father worked the grill and fryers, all the while making mental notes of how it all fit together, how to make the best use of passageways between the preparation area and the counter. My father was particularly impressed with what Tuggle had built because, as dad once told me, for all the man's achievements, he had only completed the second grade. Looking back four decades to dad's reconnaissance mission, I believe that while he accurately gauged that he was witnessing the wave of the future, he might have failed to give sufficient weight to the reality that, behind the fast-food tsunami, there existed a whole world of folks who did not want to squeeze ketchup from maddening little plastic packets onto a paper container of French fries which they were compelled to eat with their fingers. Thus it was this concept he employed in designing the prototype restaurant for his chain that would follow. And, it would be slightly flawed.

The people of Chillicothe, alerted that a Bob Evans eatery would soon arrive in their city, mistakenly believed that it would be a restaurant similar to the Gallipolis operation—a sit-down, full-service, family-oriented dining operation. They were taken aback when the ribbon-cutting ushered them into an establishment which, while carrying the Bob Evans name, was a place perhaps better described as Sausage Boy Food-o-Rama. Diners entered the restaurant, placed their orders at a counter, then proceeded to their tables. Orders were then processed by the kitchen and carried to the customers.

"The people absolutely rejected the idea," Bob Wood said. "At the end of the first week, we had done $6700 in sales. In six weeks time, we were down to $1200 a week." The place was quiet as a mortuary.

Roger Williams, who would rise to president of Bob Evans Restaurants chain, was the new kid on the block when the Chillicothe location opened. He remembered, "I was an entering freshman at Rio Grande College at the time. I had been with the company a year. When they opened the Chillicothe store, they asked me to go into management." The notion of applying a fast-food approach to marketing carry-out bags of sausage sandwiches was sinking like a bowling ball in a barrel of molasses.

"The execution wasn't bad," Williams said, "but the consumer proposition was flawed. I think Emerson might have said, 'Boys, we've got to do something, otherwise we're going to go out of business.'"

"Emerson wanted to close the thing down," an incredulous Wood still marvels 40 years after Dad's uncle attempted to pull the plug.

Dad refused. He recognized that while he had misjudged the expectations of Chillicothe diners, he wasn't ready to cut and run.

"We decided to do a very novel thing," Williams said, "which was to ask the customers what they thought. They said, 'We want to sit down and eat just like we do down on the farm at the sausage shop.'"

What followed was a change-over that transpired, largely, during one weekend.

"Friday night, I was checking out about 9 o'clock," Williams said, "and Larry Corbin called. He was the manager. He said, 'What are you doing tomorrow?' I said, 'I'm working open to close.' He asked, 'When do you have to be back in class at Rio Grande?' I told him Monday morning. He said, 'Pack your clothes.'"

Williams started work Saturday morning at 5:30, helping Corbin show the staff how to prepare the hastily adapted menu from the restaurant at the Homestead.

"We had to train everyone on the fly," Williams said. "Your dad was there. At 11:30 at night, we were still baking biscuits. At 7:50 Monday morning, I was back in chemistry class at Rio Grande, but that key weekend defined the success of Bob Evans Farms."

Once the roller-coaster transition was completed, the place was ready for customers, and they were ready for Bob Evans.

It stuns me when I consider that the number of Bob Evans Restaurants today exceeds 600. The foundation of that vast number had its roots in dad's belief that something good awaited on the other side of the hill if the board members of the company could be patient enough to allow the kinks to be excised from the concept.

"What's behind the sun?" Carl Sandburg once queried. That's the place my father was always straining to glimpse.

"Your dad never worried about the numbers," Wood said of that time. "He was a visionary."

More importantly, he knew his vision for the style of restaurant he wanted to create would catch on because the template for selling it was precisely the same as that which he used to sell sausage. He sold quality just as he had when his 69-cent-a-pound sausage was going into groceries where other brands could be had three pounds for $1. It was his old belief, "People will remember the taste long after they've forgotten the price." He also crusaded for strong product identification. He wanted his customers to understand that Bob Evans sausage was "made by a farmer on a farm." The logical transition of this image from a supermarket product to a restaurant required that the clientele be able to sense a down-home feel to the dining environment, a genuine friendliness from the staff and a wholesome goodness and value in the food set before them. Dad wanted them to feel as though they were enjoying breakfast or dinner at the kitchen table of the Homestead. He knew that it really didn't matter to the customer that he was not actually eating dinner in a farm kitchen so much as that all the trappings filled his mental appetite with a feeling suggestive of the imagined simplicity and unfettered freedom of farm life. And, of course, that simplicity was definitely imagined because the customer enjoying a wholesome meal wasn't thinking about being slapped in the face by a cow's tail at 4 a.m., staying up all night during spring lambing or all the joys of mucking out horse stalls.

Not long ago, while I was going through some of my father's old files, I came across a lined yellow tablet on which he had scribbled notes to himself. The accompanying material and clippings in the file suggested that it was of about the same vintage as the opening of the Chillicothe restaurant—1968. In his musings to himself, he had penned, "Americans are hungry for something to relate to. Farmer. Cowboy. Mythical American: A return to some sought-after freedom." It reminds me of the simple poem written by William Carlos Williams in 1924:

So much depends
upon

a red wheel
barrow

glazed with rain
water

beside the white
chickens

Honest, earthy, close to the soil. In 1968, such sentiments were sadly in short supply. The nation was in a state of epic discord and tragedy. Dr.

Martin Luther King Jr. had been assassinated in April, his death followed by the smoke and blood of riots in cities across the nation. Robert Kennedy was killed in June. Demonstrators were protesting an unpopular war in Vietnam. Violence accompanied the Democratic National Convention in Chicago. Young people were following the counter-culture's enticements to "Turn on. Tune in. Drop out." College campuses across the nation were aflame with outrage against "the establishment," a system protestors variously defined as college administrators, American business, Congress, the President or the draft. All of this was totally antithetical to everything in which my father believed. A week's worth of the evening national news could readily summon up the diverse and disturbing images of U.S. troops pinned down under fire in Vietnam, hippies sharing a bowl of smoky bliss or protestors at the White House gates.

My father knew that he wasn't doing business in a vacuum. Twenty of his customers in the inner city of Detroit—mostly mom-and-pop groceries—had been burned out in the riots of 1967. But he knew that for as much as there was a discontent across the land, there was, as well, a longing among a huge segment of the population for a return to a way of life that was recognizable, comprehensible and, occasionally, even tranquil. Make no mistake. I would not suggest here that a Bob Evans' breakfast carried anyone through the incendiary late '60s. But I believe that for many people, and my father among them, reaching for something that was rooted in a more understandable era helped sustain them through difficult times. When I am tempted to consider that some might think it blind naivete to employ one's longing, nostalgia or imagination to better endure crisis, I have to remind myself that another part of the nation was using acid, hash and hallucinogenic mushrooms to get through it.

My father understood people's yearning for a mythic hero, mythology itself having been described by the noted American psychologist Rollo May as follows: "A description of a pattern of life, arising out of the unconscious, that carries the values for a society and gives a person the ability to handle anxiety, to face death, to deal with guilt." The Greek mythology of the 20th century in the United States was the American West, the cowboy, the rancher, the farmer. All of those were romanticized, interwoven into the fabric of national pop culture—cinema, television, even advertising. Wasn't the Marlboro man (an advertising gimmick dad thought a stroke of genius) a paragon of rugged, spirited individualism, simple virtue and triumph over arduous and toilsome circumstance? Did not a part of even the counter-culture itself strike out to seize an imagined Walden in the woods or in a communal rural setting?

Thus it was into the disturbing late '60s that my father in his Stetson hat and cowboy boots, a fellow who talked plain and judged every man alike, began setting a table at which folks—like the truckers back in 1946—could take a load off, rest their elbows on the table and enjoy a little comfort food.

When my father was beginning the restaurant chain, I was finishing my college education in Colorado. I didn't get to see him as often as I wished or for as long as I would have liked. I knew, though, that he was working through a fresh challenge, and there was nothing dad savored more than climbing a new mountain. Sure, he possessed a certain amount of experience from the malt shop, the Steak House and the Sausage Shop, but building a chain presented unfamiliar obstacles. Still, he was invigorated and wide-eyed and he was ascending this untried summit in the company of the best of climbing partners—his wife.

Mom carried the responsibility of kitchen testing the recipes for menu at the first Bob Evans Restaurants. A native of the South, where food is almost a form of Holy Communion, she strived to balance delicious with wholesome and nutritious. The breakfast fare at Bob Evans was down-home: Eggs, sausage, hash browns, pancakes, waffles, biscuits. Lunch and dinner (or dinner and supper, as we say in Rio Grande) choices included made-from-scratch biscuits, country or city ham, sausage steak, smoked sausage and chicken with noodles. A variety of indulgent desserts rounded out the menu.

The early growth of the restaurant chain was, as Bob Wood described it, "a very controlled expansion." My father was willing to take risks, but they were calculated risks. The restaurant and sausage side of the business were like weights on two sides of an assayer's scale. Moving too swiftly to build new restaurants could leave the other side of the see-saw arrangement high and dry from over-capitalization. The company was not comfortable with going outside to borrow money for expansion, yet it was abundantly clear all around that despite a growing national fast-food mentality, there was also an inviting market for full-service, family-oriented restaurants serving traditional meals. My father knew that more and more women were entering the workforce, that two-income families were becoming the norm, and that these two trends augured well for offering the kind of family meal fewer people had time to prepare at home.

"I was the first real estate man they hired," recalled Howard Berry of the early days for the restaurant chain. "At the time, 1978. I was working for a developer, looking for properties to locate K-Marts. I was the first city slicker they ever hired. When I first started, we didn't want to spend more than $150,000 for a property. Because we didn't want to lease too many, we'd always want an option to buy at 15 years, in some cases for that same $150,000. Today, some of those properties, even without a building, are worth $1 million.

"We'd look for a location with a shopping center, a few motels, close to an interstate. At that time, there were Denny's, Elby's and Shoney's, but they weren't much competition. If I knew that a Shoney's and an Elby's were doing a big business, we'd go right across the street from them."

For one thing, a new Bob Evans didn't even resemble the other competition for diners; a Denny's, say, or a Waffle House. The design was the inspired genius of an architect named Coburn Morgan. Dad and Morgan got along better than their ancestors did. The architect's forebear, Civil War Confederate Gen. John Hunt Morgan had led a marauding rebel cavalry on the historic "Morgan's Raid" through Gallia County, terrorizing the countryside and stealing the good horses of an Evans' family progenitor. Coburn Morgan's creation melded his design genius with a few touches borrowed from a Scottsdale, Arizona restaurant my parents had seen while out West. The exterior was a bright barn red trimmed in white. The ascending prow of the front was crowned with a keyhole notch. Splashes of yellow combined to create a style that came to be called "Steamboat Victorian" or "Steamboat Gothic." Dad wanted a distinctive look that would separate a Bob Evans from every other business planted at an interstate exit. That wisdom had germinated in him from the days when, on family vacations, he would seek out the conspicuous orange roof of a Howard Johnsons. He knew their menu, the value to be had for his money and the consistency of the quality. It was well-lit and clean.

"I didn't want people to just drive by our restaurants," he once said.

The reception of the community where a new Bob Evans was about to open was usually more than my father or Howard Berry could hope for.

"In the early years, they begged us to come," Berry said. "They would welcome us with open arms."

One developer flatly told Bob Wood, "I'll sell this ground to you for $125,000. Burger King is willing to pay $145,000, but both my wife and I like what you do, and we are going to sell it to you because I don't want Dixie cups blowing all around my property."

Berry said that it was a bonus going into a new location to have dad on hand to welcome arriving diners. "He just had a way about him," Berry said. "He had a charisma that made people want to meet him. He was always the same guy. You could have nothing or be a millionaire. He was very considerate and caring."

When my father met people, issues of status, social position and relative degrees of economic standing neither affected nor interested him. It was that democratic side of him. He engaged them because he was genuinely appreciative of what they were doing for him by coming to eat at his restaurant. Also, dad had a deep-seated belief that most people can teach us something. He believed, as Ralph Waldo Emerson had said, "Every man I meet is in some way my superior." I need only to study a photograph from the grand opening of the Chillicothe restaurant to know the source of those personality traits. It is a festive atmosphere; red and white gingham tabletops, antique branding irons and old ox yokes on the walls. In that picture, from 1968, a couple in their sixties is seated at a table facing one another. The man is a smallish fellow with a pensive, almost taciturn appearance. He looks as though he has just remembered something important he forgot to do before he left the office. The woman, conversely, appears to be brimming with scarcely concealed enthusiasm and mirth. She looks as though she might be leaning in to catch the punch line of a joke she knows is going to be hilarious. The man is Stanley Evans, dad's father. The woman is Stanley's wife, Elizabeth, my grandmother. From the former, dad received the apprenticeship that was to be his business acumen. From his mother, he inherited his natural exuberance, a *joie de vivre* that allowed him to bring great courage and appetite to even the thorniest of problems. From her he also learned to think unconventionally. Many viewed his approach to issues or problems unorthodox, but he had come by it honestly and at an early age by combining an earnest work ethic with ingenuity. It resulted in an independence of outlook and perspective that would be with him always.

Chapter 5
A Steward of the Land

I owe much I have learned of grace and fortitude to bare trees beauti-
ful through winter's stress, and always their great tallness has renewed
and verified my faith in upwardness; so all my songs say this: that every
tree I have known lives evermore in me.

Jane H. Merchant
Listen to the Land

At the moment in my father's life when he could see the last of the
sand hastening through the hourglass, he did a thing that some folks might
think peculiar. With tablet in hand, and writing in a tentative cursive, he
began taking a census of his peonies. He moved slowly, for at 89, his step
was patient, cautious, and he knew that no one so much as himself awaited
the results of his head count. Greek mythology argues that the peony was
named for Paeon, physician to the gods, who brought the fragrant blossoms down from Mt. Olympus to share with the common world.

From my earliest recollection, my dad had been in love with peonies.
He was captivated by their flamboyant blossoms and bold hues. Poet Mary
Oliver once commended of the noble blossoms in *Peonies:*

This morning the green fists of the peonies are getting ready
to break my heart
as the sun rises,
as the sun strokes them with his old, buttery fingers

And they open---
pools of lace
white and pink---
...the flowers bend their bright bodies
and tip their fragrance to the air
and rise
their red stems holding
and there it is again---
beauty the brave, the exemplary,
blazing open.

Because peonies were a late-spring, early-summer flower, my father thought of them as made to order for Decoration Day, as Memorial Day had been called in his youth.

"C'mon," he would invite, loading his vehicle with a cargo of 3-pound coffee cans filled with peonies, "we're going to the cemetery." His weed snips in hand, armed with his 10-10-10 fertilizer and rakes, we would set out for the village of Cadmus and a nearby cemetery where his Welsh forebears had been laid to rest. He cleared the weeds and any encroaching bramble, fed the grave grass, then placed pink and red peonies at graying headstones whose etched particulars had been smoothed by time and the elements. He never sought praise or approbation for his attentions to absent kin. The only family who knew of his treks to the cemetery were those of us corralled into accompanying him on such missions. We cherished those memorable times with him and considered it an honor to help him at the graves.

Something about standing in the midst of long-departed family seemed to fill my father with a calming recognition of how the fleeting nature of mortal life fulfilled precisely the order of the seasons set forth in Ecclesiastes. Birthings and buryings, sowings and reapings. All of those milestones, whether great or small, were part of the architecture of our existence. And, to dad, they affirmed his quiet sense of comfort in the order of things. No matter how much civilization seemed to be going to hell in a hand basket at a particular moment, a trip to the cemetery put it all in perspective. Collectively, we experienced the calm that dad's family burying ground brought to him.

The cemetery bore irrevocable testament to dad's deep belief that the earth is central to all that we do. The same earth whose bounty nourished us and whose beauty sustained us also opened to receive our husks when our time had come. Because dad believed the earth to be sacred, he spent a lifetime attempting to rescue it from ill-use and neglect. More than one factor played a part in my father's stewardship of the land. He told many a newspaper reporter that the Steak House he started and the small sausage-making business that followed were merely a means to an end. He wanted to own a farm free and clear, and be able to farm it.

Dad's contemporaries may have dreamed of being firefighters, pilots or silver-screen cowboys such as Tom Mix. My father's wish was to know the land. Curiously, it was a wish that took root at a time when farming had little to commend itself to adolescent dreams. Across the U.S., in the first four years of the 1930s, the Depression had driven farm prices down 50 percent. In Iowa alone, half of all farmers had been pushed off their land by drought or economic hardship. On top of that, dust storms were so fierce in breadbasket states such as Kansas that they dimmed the sun as far east as the Appalachian Mountains. To take up farming in the midst of such adversity was a fool's errand. The situation was somewhat mitigated in Gallia County because the weather and the bankers were a little more forgiving, and most of the subsistence farmers were able to keep their families on what they grew with little concern for market fluctuations in the price of milk, or perhaps beef. Some of those small farms of 80 acres or so continued to be passed down one generation to another, though the lure of steady money to be made in the cities only hastened the rural-to-urban migration of the first quarter of the 20th century. As a consequence, the chief title holders of small farms in our area of the state were an aging population whose children had abandoned the agrarian life for other pursuits. The soil on many of those farms had been played out by inattention to crop rotation or inadequate fertilization during lean times. Yet, dad could see beauty and potential in places where others saw only impoverishment.

The hills so dear to my father had not always been wisely used by the generations that preceded him. When his forebears arrived in the Ohio country from Wales in 1840, an acre a day of woodland was being felled to make charcoal to fire crude iron furnaces. Most of the coal taken from southern and southeastern Ohio in the early part of the 19th century was being claimed by drift mines. The waste from such operations was simply heaped into mounds known as "gob piles," heaps of slag and sulfurous gas that occasionally erupted spontaneously into flames and whose runoff spelled devastation for surrounding vegetation. Large-scale strip mining arrived in Ohio as early as the year before dad was born, when one of the mammoth power shovels used to gouge out the Panama Canal was brought to Ohio to mine coal near the village of Dundee. And, just as mines played out in southern and southeastern Ohio, so too did farmland.

By the time dad's business was achieving the benchmarks that permitted him to accomplish some of the things that had been his heart's desire, Gallia County boasted an abundant supply of overworked and depleted farmland available for sale. To put it bluntly, my father's desire to acquire this land and restore it as either pasture or wildlife habitat baffled many of his neighbors. A few thought him downright unwise for wanting land so fallow, so gullied and rutted by erosion. But there was a method to his madness that could only be glimpsed if one shared his vision. Not many did.

My sister Debbie has observed, "Dad was a true believer in things that other people had given up on. I'd go out with him on the land sometimes and he would tell me, 'Now, we're going to do this and this and this with this land, then we'll let nature take care of the rest.'"

"I never went looking for land," he liked to say. "People came to me."

Once he had purchased a new parcel, perhaps a subsistence farm of 60 or 80 acres, one of his first steps was to halt continuing erosion by filling in the gullies through which topsoil was carried away during the rains. Gallia County's longtime game warden Kenny Tomlinson recalled of the next step, "He used lime to sweeten the soil. Putting the lime on also destroyed the broom sedge."

Gradually the land would be restored and dad would move on to another plot of depleted soil.

"Your dad believed you never really owned the land," Tomlinson said. "He thought it belonged to all of the people, and he believed it was his duty to make it just a little better for the next generation coming on."

Dad used to say, "I'm planting trees right now that I'll never live to see mature."

He planted japonica and lespedeza, dogwood and crab apple, hawthorn and autumn olive. He attempted to restore the American chestnut to Gallia County, the species having been virtually wiped out by a fungus in the early 20th century. By the most conservative of estimates, he planted or saw to the planting of more than 200,000 trees in his home country. That said, it must be pointed out that he was occasionally mistaken when it came to restoring the land.

Not many things in life caused dad to grit his teeth, a dead giveaway that his anger or frustration had reached the critical-mass stage. A simple little plant, the multiflora rose, could do it. My father considered it the kudzu of the North; a nuisance bush that could seem as impenetrable as the Great Wall of China. I believe that during dad's 30-year war with multiflora rose, he actually dreamed of this pesky plant. For him, multiflora rose was the stuff of nightmares. I could always tell when he had been out in No Man's Land battling it because he would return home, the skin on his arms deeply scratched and bleeding. We would treat his wounds and listen to his woes, knowing full well that he was already planning his next offensive. He never left home without clippers and a poisoning agent to do war with the plant.

The ironic fact was that dad himself had introduced multiflora rose to the land he was acquiring in hilly Gallia County because he mistakenly believed that, as in flatter northern Ohio, it could be used as a hedgerow that would serve as a windbreak for curbing soil erosion and provide a natural habitat for the grouse and the ring-neck pheasant. But, birds spread the seed and, instead of growing in straight tidy hedgerows, it grew everywhere. It dappled otherwise beautiful pasture land, and made some locations on his farm too impenetrable for deer hunting.

My father was right about one thing. The multiflora rose did provide a habitat for wildlife. And, while dad was a hunter, he spent infinitely more time making a home for game than ever he did hunting it.

My mother told me, "I remember once, it was March, it was cold. Bob said to me, 'Let's go over to the ranch and check out the Canada geese.' It was nesting time, and the drakes were very protective. They flew at the tires and batted their wings against the truck. Despite all that, we were able to get close to the nests and in this one nest we found a baby that had been orphaned. It was cold. Bob put that baby in his pocket. Now, in the barn we had a chicken brooder house. He drove nine miles to take that little bird to the chicken brooder house so it wouldn't die.

"He loved wildlife. He planted grasses that encouraged birds. He was a steward of the land. He would always say, 'There will be more people on the land, but there won't be any more land. So, let's take care of it.'"

If my father had his way, a day would have been much longer than 24 hours. Twenty-four hours made it difficult for a man trying to do everything that filled dad's agenda. Keeping his covenant with the land took time, as did his labors to restore natural wildlife habitats in his home country.

Then, too, there was always the business.

The success of the Chillicothe restaurant had been followed by the launching of another Bob Evans in north Columbus, a restaurant which, for years, routinely posted sales numbers that made it the perennial No. 1 in the chain. When two more of his restaurants opened on the east and west sides of Columbus, it was clear that dad had been onto something good when he insisted that the Chillicothe restaurant be kept open after a slow showing out of the gate. There was no particular mystique that drew customers to my father's chain of restaurants. They sold quality. They served it up in an environment as welcoming as a family reunion or a church potluck.

"Good food at a fair price in a warm, comfortable atmosphere," Roger Williams said of dad's philosophy. "If I heard your dad say it once, I heard him say it 100 times, 'The cheapest way to get rid of bad food is to throw it out. The most expensive way is to serve it to a customer.' When I was working at the Sausage Shop in Rio Grande, at the Homestead, the person who made the first pot of coffee in the morning was your dad, and he would usually throw it out. He knew that if the water had been sitting in the coffee maker overnight, some of it would have evaporated and made the first pot in the morning too strong. Throw it out.

"Your father had a clear credo," Williams said. "Quality. But I can't ever recall him getting angry to make that point. His style was more inspirational, encouraging. He would say, 'You know, if you make those hash browns just a little browner, the flavor is really going to come out in them.' He had an energy that people would feed off of. I remember I took over a store in Cincinnati that was really struggling. My first day there—first morning—the phone rang, and it was your dad."

He asked Roger, "How's it going?"

Roger proceeded to offer a rundown of several of the problems that needed addressed before the ship could be righted.

My father reassured him, "You'll take care of all of that stuff, but let me give you one thought that can guide your success the rest of your career. It's real simple. You need to treat each customer like he is the only customer you are going to have all day."

To some men, staring at the uphill side of a difficult restaurant turnaround, such advice might have seemed simplistic, dismissive, maybe even patronizing. Dad was sincere, though. He knew what Roger was up against. It would be just the thing to get Roger through that difficult period, keeping his mind off the numbers and on the customers.

Still, dad was not so much about business that he was unaware that those who helped drive the Bob Evans success story also had lives outside work. Roger not only recalls my father offering him advice on getting the Cincinnati unit out of the mire. He remembers, as well, dad showing up at the place only a few hours after Roger had just ended a long vigil at the hospital for the birth of a child. My father, recognizing that Roger looked especially fatigued, asked him what was up.

"My wife was 27 hours in labor," Roger explained.

Dad immediately replied, "Well, let's go see that baby."

He never looked at people as objects or instruments of his success. He saw them as individual human beings who—to his great fortune—had chosen to cast their professional lot with him.

"Your dad treated everybody with the same level of dignity and respect whether it was a dishwasher or a bank president," Roger said, "and I think that personality and warmth inspired what we try to accomplish in our restaurants."

Those who worked with my father over the years know that he was neither a harsh mentor nor a dictatorial tutor. Indeed, those who learned from him and succeeded within the company did so because of his enthusiasm and the vigor and imagination that colored his ideas.

"Your father would probably have had ten ideas," recalled Larry

Corbin, whose career carried him from manager of the Sausage Shop at the Homestead eventually to CEO, "and our job was to pick out one and make it work for the company. I'm kind of a nuts and bolts guy, black and white. He was more of a visionary."

"I watched everything your father did," Roger Williams said. "I remember I was once with a gentleman who was talking about his adult son. The guy said that it seemed that, when the boy was growing up, he paid no attention at all to what his father had to say. After the boy was grown, he told his dad, 'I never listened to a thing you said, but I watched everything you did.' I watched your dad a lot."

In an interview dad gave to *Restaurant Business* magazine while the chain was still in its youth, he allowed, "The restaurant business is not so hard. But you can make it hard by not taking good care of your customers. Quality must be a religion. If the hash browns are cooked improperly, throw them out. Take them off the menu. The customers may complain but they'll come back. Once you turn a customer away because of poor service or bad food, you don't get a chance to get your money back."

He continued, "Those restaurateurs who shouldn't be in the business will be weeded out in time. But I'm not worried. We take good care of our customers and they take good care of us."

Fifteen years ago, nationally syndicated *Chicago Tribune* columnist Bob Greene wrote a piece explaining not only why he was a fan of Bob Evans Restaurants but why, as well, he believed they had succeeded:

Much of what is marketed in the U.S. these days seems predicated upon the notion that Americans won't go for a product unless it is presented in some avant-garde, self-consciously off-kilter, cooler-than-thou style...Bob Evans willfully rejects this concept...The entire Bob Evans experience is designed to make customers feel as if they are welcome and at home; it is implicitly inclusionary rather than winkingly exclusionary...A simple concept: Run a place to make the customers feel it's there for them, not for you. If much of corporate and governmental America understood this, we might all be in much better shape.

If Bob Greene is right about one thing it is that Bob Evans Restaurants care deeply about what their customers think of them. From the first day the Steak House opened its doors, dad hammered home to the staff his conviction that when a diner took a seat in his restaurant a trust was established.

My father liked lists—simple, one-word-per-line prompts that he scribbled on a yellow legal pad. Each word indicated a goal about which he believed corners should never be cut. He had a short list of "musts" when it came to the restaurant business. Six endeavors occupied that roster. The first three were *quality*. The final three were known to no one, but they addressed treatment of customers. Each and every one of dad's beliefs was a crucial element in a synergism that resulted in a successful food operation. As always, dad reduced this equation down to its simplest form, the commonest of denominators.

Perhaps his concepts were the result of growing up during the Great Depression and living through the crushing poverty he and his family endured. In retrospect, I believe those lean years helped shape extraordinary men and women—the "Greatest Generation," as Tom Brokaw has aptly described them. Hard times infused them with a resourcefulness, resilience and tenacity that not only helped them win the war, but, as well, crystallized their sense of honor in dealing with others when it came to matters of business and commerce. Serving customers in a restaurant that bore my father's name was not merely a transaction, but a trust. Dad truly believed the adage which Thoreau stated so absolutely, "Goodness is the only investment that never fails."

Chapter 6
Gifts from the Golden Triangle

The heart is a millstone in a mill: when you put wheat under it, it turns and grinds and bruises the wheat to flour; if you put no wheat, it still grinds on, but then it is itself that it grinds and wears away.

Martin Luther

Within the heart is a crossroads most crucial in determining whether adversity makes us bitter or better. And, while it was the faltering of a literal heart that made latter-day millwrights of my family, it was the adventurous spirit of the figurative heart that drove the enterprise. By 1981, my father had undergone two heart surgeries and survived a heart attack. While his heedless and unflappable nature made him publicly dismissive of the gravity of that ominous trio of medical events, he was privately more circumspect. My mother was deeply worried about his health. An embolism had claimed his father at 73, and as dad approached that chronological milestone it was clear to all of us that the need for him to take the best possible care of his heart was no longer a matter about which he could be cavalier.

In the late '70s, a West Coast research nutritionist named Nathan

Pritikin emerged as one of the premier savants of human nutrition and the heart-healthy diet. Though not a physician, Pritikin's wide-ranging and innate curiosity as an inventor led him to immerse himself in diet research after he learned he was suffering from severe heart disease at 41. His diligent sleuthing ultimately unearthed a copy of a medical research study revealing that the mortality rate from heart disease and diabetes in Europe had dropped significantly during World War II despite war-time rationing and the general scarcity of food. Hardship and privation had forced European civilians to adopt a leaner, low-fat dietary regimen. Armed with the evidence from the study, Pritikin railed against the medical establishment's long-held belief that coronary disease was generally stress-related, and that its diagnosis necessitated an enforced sedentary lifestyle. His was a wildly revolutionary theory antithetical to everything that doctors had traditionally advocated. Physicians had been counseling their patients to limit their walking, avoid climbing stairs and to be sure and nap during the day. Pritikin was certain that heart disease could be largely controlled by diet and exercise, a notion that was considered medical heresy. But to that end, he opened the Pritikin Longevity Center in 1975, in Santa Monica.

Pritikin's center had been up and running six years when my parents decided to pack up and set out for a month-long stay at his dietary boot camp. The place virtually guaranteed that its visitors—if faithful to the dietary and exercise program—would not only lower their cholesterol but their weight, as well. No fat. No cholesterol. No salt. No white sugar. No caffeine. My parents learned to calculate fat grams to calories. Red meat was limited, as were shrimp and shellfish. The program was strong on lean, natural and nutritional foods. Moreover, it preached the value of consuming whole grain products that had been least altered from their natural state in order to appease the dictates of mass marketing or cosmetic appearances. Conventional bleached flour might as well be the talc on a dressing-room powder puff for all the nutritional good it was doing those who made it a staple of their diet.

"We had lectures on nutrition everyday at Pritikin," mother recalled. "Your dad lost 20 pounds and he looked great."

He might have lost more had he not discovered, during his sunrise walks from the center, a McDonald's just down the beach. He swore he never consumed anything but coffee and, truth be told, the Pritikin message had actually begun to sink in with him. By the time dad and mom returned to Gallia County, both were invigorated by the nutritional crusade of Pritikin.

The Jewell Evans who carried home from the West Coast the message of wise, heart-healthy dining was not the mother at whose farm table I had grown to adulthood. She was reared farm poor in Burke County, North Carolina. When we were growing up, there were bacon drippings in almost everything. And her food was delicious. She would always say, "Just a teensy, tiny little bit. Not enough to hurt." We always had pinto beans with cornbread made with buttermilk. The beans always included a little side meat or fatback. She added a bit of sugar to everything, justifying as she did, "Not much, now; just a wee sprinkling to bring out the flavor." Her half-runner green beans were the best in the world. But, it was the ham or bacon that served as the culinary catalyst for the superb taste.

My mother recalled of the Pritikin experience, "We came away from there feeling really well and with a good grasp of the simple truth that learning about quality and nutrition is the responsibility of everyone involved in the food process. We came back more aware of what we eat. At the Pritikin Center we learned that carbohydrates are the primary source of crucial fiber in our diets, but we place our body in a healthier state when we look towards the complex carbohydrates, good grains, fiber and bran.

"I used to think it was important to serve my family big, hearty meals. But, I've recently come to realize that the best diet is one that is balanced with those foods which are closest to their natural living state—vegetables, fruits and grains."

Looking back, I know that she was embracing this new diet because her husband's life and her own depended on it. I can also see, as well, how it could and did lead to what was to become a new family business that would bear not the name of Bob Evans, rather that of his wife. The entire venture would take on a family character, with each member eventually becoming involved in the day-to-day workings of my mother's milling operations.

To describe mother's arrival as an entrepreneur as a novel phase in her life would be unfair. For years, she had lent her kitchen-testing talent and consumer acumen to dad's business ventures. He was the first to recognize that fact, along with her ready grasp of what appealed to public taste. A scratch cook of the highest order, she could whip up something-from-nothing mealtime wonders with her eyes closed. Truth be told, she began taking a serious look at her diet long before my father did. She had experienced a carotid artery blockage and the ordeal of the surgery necessary to correct it. That, piled atop dad's coronary surgeries and ongoing cardiac episodes, convinced them that something had to be done. She didn't want to lose the man with whom she had spent four decades of her life. That love ultimately led my parents to New England and to one of the oldest and most fundamental niches in the creation of food.

By the time my parents discovered millwright Arthur Matson, he was 87 and had been grinding grain for as long as he could remember. Matson's mill, in Connecticut, was not only distinctive because of his talent and dedication, but also, and perhaps more particularly, because he milled grain using the world-renowned French buhr stones. His millstones had been quarried at Le Fert-sous-Jouarre, France. The quarry, 40 miles from Paris, had been producing the finest of millstones since before the voyage of Columbus. Granite derived there was among the hardest in the world. Infused with quartz, the igneous stone was so durable for milling grain that the same French buhrs Matson employed when he met my parents had been grinding at the time the first shot of the American Revolution was fired. His stones had likely come to the Colonies as ballast in the holds of French trading ships. Had my parents not happened upon the mill in Connecticut at the time they did, it is likely that they wouldn't have undertaken the construction of the Jewell Evans Mill in Gallia County. As fate would have it, though, arthritis and advanced age had led Matson to realize that it was time to let go of his mill. He was willing to part with six sets of French buhrs, but only with the buyer's assurance that they would be used to continue milling grain in the manner he had practiced the craft. At the time, my parents had been researching grains, mills, wheat and breads from one end of the country to the other. Sister Debbie, living in Canada at the time, pitched in to research Canadian-grown wheats. She also handled a lot of the recipe consulting. Dad and mother became self-taught experts in grains and milling, and with their pledge to Arthur Matson that they would honor his charge "to grind grain for the people," they purchased his milling stones, each pair of the six sets weighing 3400 pounds. Tractor-trailers transported the stones to Ohio where, historically, the hardest, non-French stone available during the 19th century had been fashioned from granite quarried in Vinton County and, because of its proximity to Raccoon Creek, christened the Raccoon buhr.

The construction of the mill in which the French buhrs would ultimately be located was entrusted to Mennonite carpenters from Indiana. When the so-called "Plain People" arrived to work on the mill not far from dad's first sausage plant on Hidden Valley Ranch, local residents sometimes showed up simply to watch them practice their craft. Gallia County neighbors had picnics on the grounds of the mill or spent their lunch hours watching the fascinating artisans build. They were experts at restoring old mills as well as creating the old from the new, though doing so was strenuous labor. Some of the 16-by-16 support beams for the mill weighed as much as a ton. Each had to be hand-chiseled. Wooden pegs secured all of the mortise joints and knee braces. The exterior was finished in poplar board and batten. The roof was cedar shake shingle. Setting the stones was an exacting task because each of the six sets had to be perfectly balanced.

The history of old mills records that the grinding of unbalanced wheels could easily create enough heat to set fire to the millworks. The builders set the fixed bottom stone (called a bed stone) of each set into a polished wooden hoop. Above the bed stone, the running stone was then positioned. Grain was fed from above, the adjustment of the distance between the stones determining—from coarse to talc—the texture of the finished product. In an era pre-dating precise calibration, a miller adjusted the cut of his stones by palpating the coarseness of the finished product between his thumb and forefinger, a practice some believe to have been the genesis of the expression "rule of thumb." Although mechanization, electrification and a number of improvements and inventions to move and sift the grain had streamlined the craft, milling, at its heart, had not changed much since the American millwright and inventor Oliver Evans penned *The Young Millwright and Miller's Guide* in 1795. However, it was the superior cut of the French buhr stones that allowed us to grind wheat or corn without producing nutrient-killing heat in the process. The heating and bleaching of conventional flour robs it of its natural food value and exceptional flavor. The massive steel rollers at mega-mills do not grind grain so much as they pulverize it. We wanted our wheat products to include the germ and the hull when they reached the French buhrs.

Of course, possessing the finest millstones meant little if we were grinding mediocre grain. From the outset, we decided that we would use only red spring wheat from Montana's famous "Golden Triangle" and the best Ohio-grown corn we could find. Red spring wheat, unlike winter wheat, does not lie in dormancy beneath a snow cover and is, thus, not subject to grain-crop vulnerabilities such as molds created by the combination of prolonged darkness and moisture. We grew our own buckwheat on the farm, and purchased top-quality field corn from Pickaway County farmers. The corn was air-dried in large bins to prevent cracking of the kernels which would result in a loss of flavor and nutrients.

While the pursuit of a healthier diet had compelled my parents to explore more nutritional grains for cooking and baking, the eventual out-growth of that search resulted in the inauguration of Jewell Evans Family Foods. The goal of the mill operation was to provide consumers with a wholesome array of flour, mixes and cereal, giving them a superior alternative to what was then being sold in supermarkets. Before the products were introduced to shoppers, however, it was decided that a consumer study be commissioned to gauge the market. What no one counted upon when the study was launched was that, when it comes to matters of health-ful eating and good nutritional habits, many people respond to survey questions in accordance not with how they eat but rather how they wished they could eat. Such wishful thinking, while suggesting that consumers would happily consider more nutritional products over ones that were less so, was no assurance that they ultimately would buy them. I now believe that there was also a more subtle factor at play in the survey. Women, shedding their traditional image as kitchen drones in order to make pro-fessional strides, were not eager to reclaim the June Cleaver stereotype. Notwithstanding that, some of them were torn a little by the recollection of the cooks their mothers had been while others experienced twinges of guilt that their work schedule often meant feeding their children out of fast food wrappers and pizza boxes. The result was a raft of survey responses that were bankable only in the "more perfect world" upon which they were predicated. A marketing study is not a purchase order. But, armed with a study that indicated overwhelmingly that the time was right for introduc-ing a line of more nutritional products for cooking and baking, we pro-ceeded full speed ahead.

When the wheels began turning in the family mill, my mother told a newspaper reporter, "We are proud of our mill, but we are prouder of our products because, at a time when people are reaching out for good nutri-tion, we have them.

"These are the finest whole grain products available in North Amer-ica," she continued. "We've very carefully sampled grains we wanted to mill and decided that using the hard red spring wheat would allow us to preserve the plant in its most natural state. We've spared no expense to ensure that the highest level of vitamins, fiber and flavor will be preserved in the milling process. We're using French-quarried stones that are ten times harder than the stone in most historic mills across the country. The fresh-water quartz in those stones allows the grain to remain cool throughout milling, unlike the big steel rollers of large commercial mills.

"I suppose that we could call our products health foods, but that is a term that suggests blandness to many people. I'd rather they simply be known as healthier foods."

When we entered the marketplace, the selection included whole wheat flour, corn meal, original recipe pancake mix, complete pancake mix, buttermilk pancake mix, buckwheat pancake mix, cornbread mix, hush puppy mix and 10-grain cereal. Though the product line had been christened for my mother, it was truly a family affair. She handled a lot of the recipe consulting. My job traded largely on public relations. That included everything from setting up interviews with newspaper food editors and radio talk shows to handling food demonstrations in supermarkets. My father's job was to be Bob Evans. His presence in interviews and photographs, along with his approving comments, carried a certain cachet. After all, consumers had been eating at his restaurants and purchasing his sausage products for almost 40 years. The family name was a synonym for quality. Brother Stephen was our representative in the marketplace and with purchasers. My brother Stan brought a unique talent to proving the goodness of the Jewell Evans line. He opened a bakery in Columbus' Grandview area which, using mother's whole-wheat flour, turned out some of the finest bread being produced in the nation at that time. His whole wheat, honey wheat and 10-grain cereal bread were magnificent. Instead of using preservatives, he added a touch of molasses to hold the moisture. A loaf of his whole wheat bread weighed 35 ounces, more than twice the weight of a loaf of Wonder bread. Stan was not simply the proprietor of the bakery, he was the baker, and it was backbreaking work. Although the bakery was ostensibly a retail operation, he developed a number of commercial clients—restaurants and high-end supermarkets—in the Columbus area.

My mother was particularly pleased to see Stan's bakery doing so well in Columbus because, as she recalled, "What I was actually hoping for was a bakery within the mill, a place where visitors could not only see the grain being milled, but taste and purchase the products prepared with those flours and grains. But, where the mill was located was sparsely populated, and the people weren't interested in whole grains."

She was right. In what was truly one of the great paradoxes of the business, farmers of that time had little or no interest in breads and other bakery goods prepared using the most wholesome portion of the very product they grew. When they came in from a long day in the fields, they wanted the supper table to include a tottering stack of Wonder bread. Their eating habits, though, didn't stop mother's crusading on behalf of good nutrition and healthful eating.

"We wanted to reach out to as many people as we could," she said. "I wanted Jewell Evans grains to be well received because they were revolutionary. I was so glad that we could produce something that was totally healthy. We promoted tours of the mill, and when we knew a tour was scheduled for a certain day, I would bake, using my products, and take the food to the mill so people could sample for themselves. We provided many recipes that could be prepared using our products, and I proofed every one of them in my own kitchen."

Mom's recipes included 10-grain cereal muffins; whole-wheat, chocolate-chip cookies, pioneer spice cake, 10-grain cereal bread, hush puppies and sesame crackers. The list was long enough that we published a cookbook compilation of favorites from Jewell Evans' kitchen. Her recipes were a particular hit with newspaper food editors who like to dove-tail a story on a new line of products or a new approach to nutrition with a sampling of recipes that allows readers to see for themselves.

Regrettably, it was too often easier to find the recipes in the newspaper than find the flours and mixes in the stores. Securing good, eye-level product placement in supermarkets is difficult, exasperating work. Dealing with food brokers was Stephen's role, and he poured an immense amount of time into trying to persuade conventional supermarkets that we were truly riding the curl of the wave. We were sitting on a nutritional goldmine that consumers would readily embrace if it wasn't placed before them in grocery stores at a level even with their shoe tops. Even more difficult was the business of working to convince commercial food brokers of the quality of our line.

We continued serving up our muffins or our hush puppies in supermarket demonstrations. We offered coupons whose discounts virtually wiped out our profit margin. We featured buy-one-get-one-free deals. In an effort to reach a niche of consumers that advertising surveys suggested to be committed to health and nutrition, we took out a full-page ad in *The Saturday Evening Post,* featuring a clip-out, mail-order form.

"With the mill," mother said, "I knew I was doing something that I wanted to do, and I wanted it to last. We knew the concept was good." But, business was not, and what had begun with the fire of enthusiasm and auspicious promise, in the end, became rather like a death vigil.

For a while, the mill continued to produce the grains Stan used in his bakery operations. The commercial success of his breads served as an affirmation of the message we were trying to get across with our marketing efforts. The visual acuity of hindsight being what it is, I can look around at today's health-food and high-end supermarkets such as Whole Foods and Wild Oats and know that we were less in the curl of the wave than out in front of it. In the end, we simply had to yield to the reality that we could not sustain the operational overhead of a mill that had become a non-profit venture.

Chapter 7

The American Quarter Horse, an American Champion

The wind of heaven is that which blows between a horse's ears.

Arabian Proverb

My father liked to say, "If you want to double your money in the horse business, just fold it." Yet, for whatever occasional ill-advised investments he might have made buying and breeding those noblest of beasts, nothing under the sun could have persuaded him to surrender that consuming passion. Like Winston Churchill, he believed that the outside of a horse does something wonderful for the inside of its rider. Right near the top of a mile-long list of gifts my father gave me is the love of horses. He never had a horse as a child and, while it would be folly to read too much into that small parcel of his past, I can't help but wonder if that fact didn't fuel his affection when he became a man. It likely had more than a casual bearing on his decision that his own children ought to have a pony. Just how we survived that ill-tempered little pony named Candy is something of a wonder, but, in the end, I suppose, she whetted our appetite for riding.

Once we moved to the Homestead, horses were always around. We used them to cut cattle and to move dad's Charolais from pasture to pasture. They were a pleasant diversion when dad wanted to entertain guests from the city with a trail ride. But, because my father believed that a horse ought to earn its feed, he was partial to the American Quarter Horse breed.

Today, if you travel to Columbus during the first three weeks of October, you will doubtless see your share of Stetsons, boots and denim. The annual All American Quarter Horse Congress is the largest, single-breed horse show in the world. It draws 650,000 people to Columbus and infuses the Central Ohio economy with a whopping $110 million windfall each autumn. More than 8,500 horses are transported to the city, including the prized studs who qualify to occupy Million Dollar Stallion Avenue. The competitions for reining, roping and cutting play to packed houses. The congress is also a stop on the Professional Bull Rider Tour, the Formula 1 of rodeo. When I consider the event today, it is difficult to believe that, in 1967, when the Ohio Quarter Horse Association first decided to hold the congress they did so only with the provision that they would scrap the whole idea if they couldn't raise the $10,000 needed to get it off the ground.

For all of the glitz, glory and big money that the event has become, I never glimpse the convergence of an impressive convoy of horse trailers into the city that I don't think about a feisty, wiry, little horse trainer my father crowned with the nickname "Pee Wee."

Leo "Pee Wee" Barbera was not born to pasture, paddock and stable. One of a half-dozen children of an Italian steelworker in Canton, he earned his first ride by mucking out stables for a family that kept ponies. By 15, and at a whopping 92 pounds, he was jockeying Quarter Horses on a dirt track near Waynesburg, Ohio, and pumping gas to keep a little change in his pocket. He was serving up high-test one summer day near Canton when a Chevy station wagon pulled up to the pump, and a 40-something fellow in a Stetson and string tie rolled down the window. My father's friendship with Pee Wee began with four words: "Fill 'er up, son."

"Who was that guy?" Pee Wee inquired of his boss after the station wagon departed.

"That's that sausage guy," came the reply.

Little known to Pee Wee or dad, their ultimate friendship had already been sealed by their mutual affection for Quarter Horses.

The Quarter Horse, fittingly, is a distinctly American breed, for just as the singular strength of this nation was founded upon the vast diversity of those who settled it, the Quarter Horse traces its lineage to a variety of ancestors. When the Colonies were being settled, the favored horse of the leisure class was the English Thoroughbred. Tall and sleek, it was better suited for pleasure than plow. However, long before the U.S. declared its independence from Great Britain, Colonists had begun to experiment with cross-breeding English horses with those that were already in the Americas well before the landing at Plymouth Rock. Native Americans had cultivated the Chickasaw horse from stock whose ancestry could be traced back to Iberian, Barb and Arabian breeds. Although Quarter Horses may have been bred and refined for work on ranches and farms, the breed took its name from the horse's considerable gift as a sprinter. In a quarter-mile race, they were impossible to beat. The nickname "Quarter Miler" ultimately gave way to "Quarter Horse" and with it successive efforts to perfect a breed worthy of the title "America's Horse."

The Quarter Horse's attributes in racing were readily matched by its adaptability to the needs of ranching and farming. The animal had an intuitive grasp of how to work cattle. Agile, quick learners, they possessed incredible endurance. Their physical characteristics included powerful, broad chests and rounded, well-muscled rumps. Ranchers learned that they could work a Quarter Horse all week and still compete with the horse on the weekend in reining, cutting, roping and barrel-racing events. Much of the generational fine-tuning of the breed transpired in Texas at some of the larger ranches. In particular, I recall that early on in my father's horse-breeding ventures, he occasionally traveled to the storied King Ranch in Texas. He had an innate sense about breeding, whether cattle or horses, and was willing to take the time to research the breed registry, a ponderous *Who's Who* among the equine community. To the extent that my father knew what made a good horse, he knew, as well, what made a good trainer, and his chance meeting with "Pee Wee" Barbera would prove a fortunate one for both.

Pee Wee had an innate affinity for training and showing horses, a natural command of the animal that predisposed it to oblige his coaxing and cajoling, along with all the practice and training necessary to get a horse ready to show at halter or in more vigorous competition.

The writer Michael Korda summed up horse people and described "Pee Wee's" soul-mate connection with the equine breed when he wrote of horses and riders in his book *Horse People*.

Horses aren't mind readers, but it's pretty clear that the rider's attitude signals itself to the horse. A self-confident, determined attitude communicates itself to the horse, and so, unfortunately, does a fearful, uncertain, and mentally unprepared one.

No telepathy is involved—it's simply that the horse is superbly equipped by Mother Nature to respond instinctively to small signals, which is to say that when you're riding, your breathing, your rate of perspiration, your level of anxiety, and your pulse rate are all being communicated constantly to the horse, which draws from all these things its own conclusion about what is going on up there in the drivers seat.

In time, Pee Wee would help dad notch one of his greatest successes with horses, but, when two first met, dad was merely doing his part pitching in to try to help keep the fledgling Ohio Quarter Horse Association a solvent and viable agency. The inception of the OQHA had its genesis in 1949, near Canal Fulton where a small knot of horsemen were sitting around engaged in horse talk when one of their number introduced the topic of the improving the popularity and awareness of the American Quarter Horse. One of those present was an Oklahoma transplant named George Pfaltzgraph, who was only too happy to show the others his horse, Chili, one of the first Quarter Horse stallions brought to Ohio from out West. Then and there at the meeting, the men decided to form an association for the promotion of the breed. There was nothing auspicious or ostentatious about the maiden meeting of the group in 1951. The first president Al Zaleski later recalled for a silver-anniversary scrapbook of the All American Quarter Horse Congress:

It took place not in the glitter of a magnificent assembly hall with an air of grandeur, but in the humblest of surroundings. To say that the meeting place smelled was to cast no reflection on the owner or the conditions of the surroundings. However, many succeeding meetings of the Ohio Quarter Horse Association were held at the F.W. Renner tallow and slaughtering plant. The odors that struck one's nostrils when approaching the plant were a confusing mixture of rendered tallow, cattle and meat scraps. Saddle tacks lined the room along the side. The tack trunks and miscellaneous equipment took so much room that it left little space for sitting. A card table was set up in one end of the room. There was a strong scent of leather in the air and it added nostalgia to this historic, never-to-be forgotten meeting

Each of the dozen men present kicked in an initial $80 membership fee. In the group's early years, Springfield's Nancy Folck, who was instrumental in the founding of the association, recalled recently, "At the time, the Ohio Quarter Horse Association didn't even have enough money to buy a typewriter. I had to write out the minutes of the meeting in longhand."

In the late 1950s and early 1960s, Nancy Folck's husband, Blair was emerging as one of the association's most crucial directors. Like dad, Blair raised Charolais cattle and was primarily interested in promoting and refining the Quarter Horse because it was such an essential and valuable breed for farm work.

The first Bob Evans trail ride of the Ohio Quarter Horse Association took place the last week of September in 1961. The purpose was purely to allow Quarter Horse folk a chance to get away for a weekend in Rio Grande. My parents served up a chicken dinner for 275 and brought in a band called the Holland Hotshots, who played for both round and square dances.

The early '60s were a pivotal time in my family's interest in Quarter Horses for a couple of reasons. Not only did my father have a vigorous interest in seeing the breed developed and showcased more throughout Ohio and the Midwest, it was also an avocational interest he could pursue in the company of his children, all of whom were captivated to one degree or another by horses.

Dad wanted something more for us than to simply have hobby horses. We rode like crazy on the Homestead helping dad drive cattle to different pasture fields, checking foals and mares and fences, but I believe that he really wanted us to test ourselves on horseback. At the time, I was 14 years old, my older sister, Gwen, 16, and Debbie, 12. I suppose that each of us had our own personal reasons for wanting to hit the horse-show circuit with dad. He was always great traveling company. He was up for anything and a super trooper. So, even if we had to load up the trailers at 2 a.m. to light out from Rio Grande--like some fly-by-night circus trying to skip town--we knew that an absolute adventure awaited us just beyond the next set of small town lights. We would chatter until boredom set in, then sing for a while to kill time. Dad had great stories to tell about his ancestors, military school and some of the ornery pranks he pulled off as a boy. He gave us tips, too, on driving, horseback riding and handling horses. He would talk about whom he thought knew the most about Quarter Horses and whom he respected. We listened to every word he uttered on those trips. I think those times were special for Gwen, Debbie and me because it was one of those rare occasions when we had our father completely to ourselves. If mom was in the car, he only had eyes for her.

The big event during that era was the Midwestern Open. It always took place in late June. We practiced all year just to get ready for it. I barrel-raced a horse named Popeye at the time, a black, Arabian Quarter Horse who would become so excited at the prospect of the race that the whites of his eyes showed, and someone had to hold him by the bridle until we were off and running. If you were a true hell-bent-for-leather barrel racer, you were willing to tear yourself up just for a trophy. Some girls actually broke their shin bones on the barrels. You had to pick up your final speed by flying down that final stretch. Yet, a few times I caught myself trying to hold Popeye back. Finally, when someone pointed that out to me. I immediately sold him to a woman who made him a state champion barrel racer. However, I wasn't completely star-crossed. At 18, I captured the Ohio State Fair's all-around youth trophy for reining, horsemanship and pleasure, beating more than 280 contestants, including some of the best youth riders I knew. I respected them immensely, so I was in shock when I won.

We attended all the shows with dad. Sometimes the events would not end until 2 a.m., with the cutting horse competition saved for last. He would stay for every minute of it, including a mesmerizing chance to witness the antics of a "one-eyed" cutting horse named Rey Jay who could usually put the balance of the competition to shame. Rey Jay, truth be known, was not actually blind in the eye that was kept covered when he was competing in the ring. He had a severe case of dry-eye syndrome that prevented the tear duct from washing the grit from an eye while he was in the midst of an event. Hence, the eye was kept sheathed with an open-ended funnel cover that allowed Rey Jay to see out of a small peep-hole at the end while preventing dust irritation and distracting the horse in the heat of competition. Rey Jay won his share of events, though was not uncommonly docked judging points because of his pesky little habit of biting calves on the nose to keep them in line.

For my father, one of the most memorable chapters of his introduction into the Quarter Horse movement was a beloved little mare named Poco Red Queen. According to the Quarter Horse registry, her lineage was legitimized by her affiliation with the foundational steed Poco Bueno, out of Texas, and on her mother's side the great sire, Red Ant, out of Cincinnati and owned by Herb Heekin. She was solid sorrel, stood 15 hands and had a regally defined confirmation. The trainer who rode her to the National Pleasure Championship of the United States in 1963 was none other than "Pee Wee" Barbera, the novice, teen-age trainer who had once pumped gasoline for dad up near Canton and asked of the departing "sausage man," "Who was that guy?"

"Pee Wee" and my father would become lifelong friends, and while the former raced, reined, roped and trained all manner of Quarter Horses, Poco Red Queen was the mare he rode when she captured first-place honors for world-champion, pleasure Quarter Horse. In one of the old annuals of the All-American Quarter Horse Congress is featured a wonderful old photo of "Pee Wee" and dad standing next to Poco Red Queen. She is sleek as any Quarter Horse ever stood. My father is wearing a buff pair of khakis and a Stetson set in a slightly rakish style atop is head. Pee Wee, diminutive by comparison, is at his left. Poco Red Queen was not a large horse by Quarter Horse standards, so she and Pee Wee were a match made in heaven.

Reflecting on those days, "Pee Wee" would remember, "At that time, no one knew whether the Ohio Quarter Horse Association would be successful or whether the congress would become the best and greatest Quarter Horse Show in the world. But your father was involved in all of that."

In the process of dad's involvement with the Ohio Quarter Horse Association, he and my mother became quite good friends with Blair and Nancy Folck, who were both instrumental in the formative years of OQHA. Both of our families raised Charolais cattle, and it was during a joint foray to the national Charolais congress, the Kansas City Royal, that an idea was hatched that was destined to change the Quarter Horse world forever. Watching the proceedings at Kansas City, Blair and my father mused about what such a livestock congress might do for Ohio if Quarter Horses could be showcased in the same manner as Charolais. Excited about the prospect, they brought the idea back to the next meeting of OQHA expecting an enthusiastic response from other board members. The Silver Anniversary edition of the All-American Quarter Horse Annual recalled of that stormy meeting at which Blair and dad tried to sell the idea, "Many torrid and testy discussions took place at a directors meeting. A few board members argued that the association had a bank account holding the princely sum of $3,500 which was far too little to risk on a foolhardy adventure such as a major statewide Quarter Horse exhibition." A few directors groused among themselves that the idea of the show seemed merely to be an opportunity to hold a horse sale for Blair. Disagreeing, dad argued that a horse show or sale held purely for the purpose of selling and showing would be of no long-term profit to the association. He added, however, that the idea that the show could succeed if combined with clinics conducted by the Ohio State University College of Veterinary Medicine to educate horse breeders on the latest techniques and advances in equine medicine. When the most stubborn of the opponents to what would become the All-American Quarter Horse Congress refused to risk the paltry treasury on hazarding such an event, Blair Folck proposed raising $10,000 in sponsorship monies over a six-month period with the proviso that any losses sustained in the process of doing so would be borne exclusively by him and Bob Evans. Dad stood behind Blair on the vote and out of such a fragile beginning was launched an event that today is the fourth largest convention in the world and the third largest in the United States.

A few years before Blair's death and not many before that of my own father in 2007, the two men attended the All-American Quarter Horse Congress in Columbus. Looking around at the sea of faces and the hundreds of horses brought to the city to compete in all of the major events that are now part of the show, dad turned to Blair and marveled, "The city of Columbus owes you a big favor."

Indeed, it did, but it was just like dad to take none of the credit for himself. He could not have cared less about the accolades.

Chapter 8
Home Country Scholars

Education is a companion which no misfortune can depress, no crime can destroy, no enemy can alienate, no despotism can enslave.

Joseph Addison

Wayne White was a young man just getting started in his Lawrence County hometown of Greasy Ridge when President Lyndon B. Johnson came to Appalachia in April, 1964 to promise to wage war on the poverty so commonplace in the region. He visited the people of Kentucky, West Virginia, southern Ohio and other states whose fortunes had too long been tethered to the meager incomes to be made working mines that had played out or trying to survive on subsistence farms. Many of those trying just to get by were rearing children whose birthrights were little more than the lot of their parents. When LBJ arrived in Kentucky to make his landmark announcement, he promised the governors of the nine-state Appalachian Regional Council that he would seek no less than $250 million to fire the first shot in his battle against poverty in Appalachia.

Almost a half-century after LBJ's promise, the states which had been determined to be a part of American Appalachia—29 of Ohio's counties

115

among them—still struggle to find decent-paying jobs and to create for their children a better life than they had for themselves. Although LBJ's proposed war on poverty in Appalachia was well-intentioned, the lion's share of the funding to assist the area was geared at infrastructure improvement, highway access and assistance to the coal industry. More than four decades after the President's pledge to bring assistance to the nine states immersed in poverty in Appalachia, ample evidence exists that LBJ didn't succeed much more with his War on Poverty than he would with his War in Vietnam.

Yet to this day, McDowell County, West Virginia, the Mountain State's equivalent of Wayne White's native Lawrence County, does not have one consecutive mile of four-lane highway. Without jobs to hold young people to their native soil, along with strong and persistent encouragement to attend college once they have completed high school, it makes little difference whether the roads of Appalachia are one-lane or four—they all lead away from home.

Wayne White was four years out of Waterloo High School when LBJ came to Appalachia. Like many of his classmates from the Greasy Ridge area, he had cast a longing look at the mines, mills and factories along the Ohio River awaiting many graduating seniors from Lawrence County. He had been willing to give college a try, but just couldn't see how some hick from Greasy Ridge might fit in with a more sophisticated and cosmopolitan college crowd. Noting that White was a cut above in spirit, character and academics, his high school principal Kenneth McCauly leaned on the young man to apply for a scholarship to study elementary education.

McCauly spoke bluntly to White, reminding the boy, "Just because you're from Greasy Ridge, you don't have to live up to the stereotypical reaction that name might create rolling over the tongue of some college admissions director."

In the end, White applied for and landed a scholarship. After earning his degree, he returned to teach at Waterloo High School. After 30 years as teacher and administrator, he retired in 1992. But, a second career was just beginning at the urging of another child of Appalachia: Bob Evans.

Wayne White and my father shared a lot in common. They grew up tough, scrappy, proud, industrious, inventive and—yes—a little on the mischievous side. Both men were plain-spoken and straightforward. While my father's high-school performance at Gallia Academy left much to be desired, he had improved his school work at Greenbrier Military School and—but for his migraine headaches—might well have finished his studies at the Ohio State University College of Veterinary Medicine.

When White's high school principal challenged him to rise above the stereotypes surrounding the Wayne Whites and Bob Evanses of Ohio hill country, the Waterloo graduate did just that.

White and my father put their heads together not long after dad was appointed to the Ohio Board of Regents, the body of executors who oversee the conduct of the college and university community within the state of Ohio. Wayne and dad were of like mind and kindred heart on one central point about educating children from Appalachia. It had to be made a priority, and it had to be achieved by overcoming in some high school students self-deprecating and self-defeating attitudes about their roots and the value of college. Dad wanted to push for it, and he knew Wayne White was the perfect man to get it done.

Speaking from his own youth, White conceded, "The experiences of an Appalachian student don't match those of a student from Dublin, Ohio. We were aware that city folks had better clothes and an easier life in terms of physical work. I think there was a self-consciousness about being very rural, very remote and having less than others. Yet students who see that college can be an option for them have hope. Your life doesn't have to end with high school."

Brenda Haas, who is today the executive director of the Ohio Appalachian Center for Higher Education founded by my father and Wayne White, learned when she took the job that while an average of 30 percent of high school seniors from Appalachian Ohio went on to attend college, the national average was 62 percent.

"Yet 80 percent of our students were saying that they wanted to attend," Haas said. "We found that the main barriers were low self-esteem, lack of information and poverty. Many of them didn't think they could afford it. We're talking about youth who would have been the first in their families to attend college. The great tragedy is that some of the barriers are perceived barriers. They were smart enough to attend. They didn't have information, and sometimes role models weren't there. They are very hard-working, creative and resourceful young people. They have a pride in their culture. True, sometimes they can be wary of outsiders. Sometimes it is very hard to ask a question because in the asking of it you are disclosing to others that you just don't know.

Dad and Wayne calculated that the program would run most efficiently when high school teachers and administrators became, essentially, advocates for their students; when they pushed college visits, college fairs and rewarded the achievements of their university-bound students.

When dad and Wayne launched OACHE in 1993, one of the first high schools to receive a grant to promote college attendance was Newcomerstown, in Tuscarawas County. During the six-year period from 1993 to 1999, the number of high school seniors who planned to attend college jumped from 28 percent to 80 percent. In one four-year period at Newcomerstown, the number of students taking the ACT doubled.

Not every school posted such a stellar showing as the program got underway. In Pike County, Waverly High School's increase in college-bound students grew by only 5 percent. Yet before OACHE was even a decade old, the Washington-based Public Employees Roundtable evaluated the program and confirmed "that the college-going rate has increased in 77 percent of the projects, with a mean increase of 16 percent." The Roundtable cited those figures when it named OACHE as one of only seven programs at all levels of government to win the Public Service Excellence

Award for 2001. OACHE also captured an award as semifinalist in 2000 for the Innovations in American Government Awards bestowed by the John F. Kennedy School of Government at Harvard University.

OACHE works because my father and Wayne believed that to achieve a goal in Appalachia you don't need a bureaucrat in Washington to throw buckets of money at it. Nor did either man feel it was necessarily in the best interest of getting Appalachian high school students to grasp the importance of college by establishing a massive, monolithic federal bureaucracy to push such a program. Central to the message of Wayne and my father was the simple truth: "If these two old Appalachians could do it, we know that all of you can, as well."

Readers will recall that in the Introduction to this biography of my father, I recounted the story of an assistant occupational therapist named Jill Sullivan. A product of Coal Grove, Ohio, not too distant from Wayne White's own Greasy Ridge, she grew up making her own way in life, earning her own keep. She mowed lawns, mucked out stables, washed cars, ran errands—anything to turn a dollar and help realize her dream of attending college. While she was a high school senior it sadly dawned on her that she simply did not have enough money to pay for the first two semesters at Shawnee State College. She confided this dilemma to Wayne White who, in short order, called her to his office and handed her a business envelope stuffed with cash. She never knew until she had completed her college studies and was working at Holzer Hospital taking care of my father following his stroke that he had been her anonymous benefactor. And, there she was, taking care of a very sick man who had authored her greatest living wish. That, as much as anything, is what OACHE is about.

A few months ago, my family was invited to a meeting of the Appalachian Regional Commission in Virginia for the presentation of a posthumous award being bestowed in my father's honor. I attended the event in the company of my mother, my sister Debbie and brothers Stan and Steve. None of us were sure what to expect when the Appalachian Regional

Commission's Co-Chair Anne Pope rose to deliver a few remarks in conjunction with the honor being bestowed.

"Bob Evans was a true child of Appalachia," she began. "His life offers an inspiring example of both business, success and a commitment to giving back to the region. When I think of Bob Evans, what I think of—in addition to many a good breakfast—is education. Bob Evans was passionate about education—about the importance of education in Appalachia. Together he and Wayne White pioneered the Ohio Appalachian Center for Higher Education, OACHE as we affectionately call it, an innovative approach for boosting the percentage of high school students in Appalachian Ohio who go on to college. This program even caught the eye of Harvard's Kennedy School of Government, which a few years ago gave the program its Innovations in Government Award, carrying a cash award of $100,000. Wayne White had the vision for OACHE. Bob Evans provided the money for that vision. And as Congressman Hal Rogers of the House Appropriations Committee often comments, 'A vision without money is just a hallucination'. But perhaps most importantly, Bob Evans believed in Wayne and his vision, providing constant encouragement, pushing the state legislature for state funding, and putting his reputation behind the program. His commitment to education wasn't limited to just Appalachian Ohio. Funding that Mr. Evans provided helped maintain the college-going program in neighboring West Virginia. Mrs. Evans and the rest of the family, I've considered it my mission to try to take what Wayne and Mr. Evans created and spread it to all of Appalachia. We've now grown your college-going program to 10 centers in 9 states, and last year more than 11,000 students participated in it. And we're not finished yet. We're grateful to the entire family for your belief in, and contribution to, this wonderful region called Appalachia. So I believe that our organization could not have picked a more deserving person for this inaugural Humanitarian Award than Bob Evans."

The entire hall rose as one to honor my mother and celebrate the memory of dad. The ARC presented mom with a hand-painted oil lamp whose artistic motif was a rendering of the Homestead.

Regrettably, both my father and Wayne White are now gone. But, OACHE continues to assist high school students in the 29 counties of Ohio Appalachia with their hearts set on attending college. One of the bolder, more recent programs of OACHE is its recently inaugurated "Seniors to Sophomores" program to assist high school students earn their first year of college credit while they are still attending high school. The program, new to many of OACHE's constituents and cited during the 2008 State of the State address by Governor Ted Strickland, permits a student from Appalachia to enroll simultaneously in high school while also enrolling in an accelerated learning program such as Advanced Placement, College Tech Prep, International Baccalaureate, or the traditional Secondary Enrollment Option Program."

The governor also pledged during his address to offer associate and bachelor's programs in core fields available in a university setting within 30 miles of every Ohio high school student.

The role that my father played in what OACHE has become today was perhaps best summed up by my nephew Bart Kayser, who said of dad, "All he wanted was to give those kids the tools to realize their dreams. He wanted to give them a fighting chance."

Chapter 9
Dad's True North:
Saving the Family Farm

*A person who undertakes to grow a garden at home, by practices
that will preserve rather than exploit the economy of the soil, has his mind
precisely against what is wrong with us...What I am saying is that if we
apply our minds directly and competently to the needs of the earth, then
we will have begun to make fundamental and necessary changes in our
minds. We will begin to understand and to mistrust and to change our
wasteful economy, which markets not just the produce of the earth, but
also the earth's ability to produce.*

Wendell Berry

Halfway through the decade of the 1980s, America and the world
were awash with a groundswell of music concert efforts aimed at focus-
ing people's attention on world hunger, apartheid, AIDS, racism and U.S.
foreign adventurism in Central America. We had Band Aid, Live Aid. A
vast chorus of singers poured hearts and voices into *We Are the World* a
musical plea for compassion that became, for a while, the global anthem

attempting to persuade its listeners that we are all one people fighting everything from starvation to homelessness.

After lending his support to a number of the epic musical events designed to raise funds and focus the attention of the world on its festering sores, country artist Willie Nelson, whose childhood backyard was six miles of furrowed fields between the towns of Abbott and West, Texas, decided it was time to do something about the plight of the family farmer.

Willie may not have been as eloquent as Wendell Berry in articulating the inestimable value of the America's farmers and stewards of the land, but when he began assembling his cast for the first Farm Aid concert in the fall of 1985, he said, "I've always believed that the most important people on the planet are the ones who plant the seeds and care for the soil where they grow. We're fighting for the small family farmer, which means that we're fighting for every living American."

Dad never met Willie Nelson, but in a fundamental and compelling way, they had almost simultaneously embarked on crusades to save the family farm.

From 1980, until the mid '90s, almost 1million farmers were driven from their land because of the combined problems of depleted crop prices, tumbling land values, skyrocketing interest rates and accumulated debt. Author Joel Dyer, in his book, *Harvest of Rage*, pointed out that a study conducted in rural America from 1981 to 1988 revealed, as he noted, "That more farmers died from suicide than from any other unnatural cause…In some areas of the country, equipment accidents, which had long been listed as the number one cause of farm deaths, were being outpaced by suicides at a staggering ratio of 5:1."

An Oklahoma agriculture support group called Ag-Link was running a suicide prevention hotline, and there was no shortage of clients. Farmer Cletus Blabough, of Ponca City, Oklahoma, communicated, "I am writing this letter to let you know why so many farmers in this area are shooting themselves. One year ago I had a gun to my head and was going to end it all. I called the hotline to see if I could find help. A very nice lady who had lost her husband the same way was very understanding and helped me see there was light at the end of the long tunnel of misfortune." In the midst of all of this, and with Willie Nelson, Neil Young, Johnny Cash, Bob Dylan, John Mellencamp and others mounting the stage to a packed stadium in Champaign, Illinois, my father had been quietly setting in motion a plan of action to keep the family farmer on his farm. It was the key to staving off foreclosures and ending the cycle of spiraling debt for expensive new equipment. On the cusp of dad's retirement from the company, he became a champion for the cause of year-round grazing.

"If I had known the secret of year-round grazing," he told me as he was shaving one morning, "I never would have gotten into the business of making sausage." He meant it, and I was astounded.

For eight years my parents had been spending a couple months each winter in Arizona. But when dad made up his mind to try to sell farmers on the idea of year-round grazing, my mother remembered, "He had been sitting up nights figuring things out. He said, 'I don't want to come here anymore. I want to sell the house. I want to give the rest of my life to year-round grazing.'"

In the midst of his crusade, my father told a reporter for *Cooperative Farmer,* "Farmers are the foundation of this whole country. I hate to see these young people, these farm boys that have a tremendous work ethic and are the backbone of the nation to be driven off the land."

At the heart of dad's activism and passion for saving the family farm was a taproot belief that there was something good, wholesome and of inestimable value in growing up on a farm. He was not only concerned about the farmers who were working the land in the mid-80s and into the '90s. He was concerned about their children, heirs to the vocation if they chose. He was trying to keep youngsters on the land of their heritage instead of packing up for the big city only to discover that many large businesses were laying people off and outsourcing jobs overseas. Without a college education, these young people faced options that often came down to flipping burgers or stocking the shelves at Wal-Mart.

My father wanted them to stay on the farms. He believed they had much to give and could run successful operations using the theories of intense-management grazing in cow-calf operations instead of having to put up a huge outlay for the farm equipment necessary for baling, combining and storing forage for winter feeding.

"This wasn't a passing fancy with your father," my mother recalled of his campaign on behalf of year-round grazing. "He really believed deeply in his heart he was doing something to help save the family farm. He didn't like to see the young people leaving the family farm for the city. He felt it weakened the family circle."

At the same time that dad began waging his battle to help save family farms, a commission in Oklahoma was taking testimony from people who had lost theirs. The testimony of a 9-year-old girl from Tonkawa, Oklahoma conveyed the story of what the crushing of the family farm does to the children involved. She told the commission:

About one and a half years ago, my family lost its farm. I had many losses before we lost our farm. Like my horse died, and that hurt me a whole lot. I didn't stop crying for two days. Then my dog got ran over and I thought he was going to die, but he lived. Then we had to give away our cats and kittens.

It was a lot of pressure when we lost our farm. It was sad to lose. After the farm was repossessed, it was very hard to change schools since I went to school there my whole life. When I went to the new school I cried almost every day.

"There is no way for farmers to make it if they don't go to year-round grazing," dad told a reporter. "We'll find grasses somewhere in the world— it doesn't make a darn where-and we'll go after them. It's going to take several years, but we know we can do it." To prove his point, dad wintered over 50 Charolais cows and their calves without feeding them any stored winter forage or grain. He routinely moved them from one of four pastures to another as the grasses became grazed out.

David Zartman, professor of animal science at The Ohio State University, explained that a four-pasture arrangement for intense- management grazing is an involved process slightly complicated in layman's terms but, he explained simply, might include in one pasture K-31 tall fescue year-round. A second pasture might be white or red clover. The third could be perennial rye grass mixture. The fourth might be Kentucky bluegrass.

Both my father and Zartman spent time in New Zealand exploring grazing there because of that country's reputation as one of the world's best in management intensive grazing. Meanwhile, back at the Farm Aid concert, John Mellencamp was singing:

Rain on the scarecrow, blood on the plow
This land fed a nation, this land made me proud
And son I'm just sorry there's no legacy for you now
Rain on the scarecrow, blood on the plow.

"Year-round grazing," Zartman said, "is ecologically sound, is environmentally sound, and it has a good potential to be profitable. Management-intensive grazing requires very little machinery, though it is not a simple or haphazard concept," as resonated by Wendell Berry in the preface to this book.

"Your dad lobbied hard for more support for year-round grazing. He was always challenging the current systems in place. We put together a 4H project book demonstrating to young people how they could try their hand at the concept. He generated a scholarship program for young people who were doing the grazing project as part of their 4H work. That was his attempt to attract kids to grazing. He was asking himself as he did this, 'How do you keep bright young people in southern Ohio?'"

Working in conjunction with OSU's agricultural research center in Wooster, the University established a farm near Canfield, Ohio for a demonstration of the potential advantages of management-intensive grazing.

They placed a mixed herd of Jerseys and Holsteins on a 30-acre farm to see if they could succeed there with year-round grazing. "We didn't completely achieve year-round grazing, but we came pretty close," Zartman said of the experiment.

Hundreds of family farms were going into foreclosure every month, which renewed dad's passion and sense of mission that he could help stave off the dwindling of family farms. The message was his gospel, and he preached it to anyone who would listen at any hour of the day or night, any day of the week. But, he was waging a war against entrenched resistance on two fronts.

"Farmers are stubborn," Zartman said, "or they wouldn't be farming. And, they are risk-adversive. They've got so much risk in their lives already. They would tell us, 'It will work for the Amish, but how about us regular farmers'."

Many of those farmers knew no other way of farming with cattle than confinement farming. They had put themselves in debt to buy expensive baling equipment and combines. If they were to convert to year-round grazing, much of the equipment they owned would sit idle. Moreover, Zartman suggested, farmers are highly subject to the attitudes and reactions of their agricultural contemporaries. They didn't want to be the first to try out a concept they weren't convinced would work. They were locked into a vicious farm economy cycle that has been described by Ronald Jager in *The Fate of Family Farming* thusly, "Simplified, the cycle looks like this: increased farming efficiencies lead to higher production, which often leads to oversupply and lower commodity prices, which drives farmers to higher efficiencies, which leads to higher production, which leads to lower commodity prices, which drives farmers to higher efficiencies...and so the cycle goes. That is why farmers get bigger or get out."

Dad wanted The Ohio State University's Department of Animal Sciences to come out full-bore in favor of year-round grazing. It could save farms he argued, and keep young people on land that had been passed on one generation to another for years.

"Why didn't we go out full-bore?" Zartman asked when it was all over. "By and large, the faculty didn't believe in it. And if the faculty was against it, so would be the administrators."

Universities receive grants and gifts and opportunities to participate in research projects from benefactors who have a business interest in agriculture. If their niche of conventional farming—selling farm equipment, say—were compromised by a sudden change in techniques of farming as a result of a bold university stand, they might be disinclined to continue their role as patrons of the offending college department. Dad was crushed by the university's failure to challenge entrenched conventions and procedures. Zartman lamented, "We were turning our backs on the chance to help farmers who were not high-tech based, but who just wanted to be farmers."

One of Zartman's disciples was a dairy farmer in Logansport, Indiana, who just happened to hear the professor speak at a seminar he attended. Dave Forgey had never wanted to do anything but farm. He explained, "I had a conventional dairy and milked in a conventional confinement system; about 280 Holsteins in our milking herd. We had bunker silos and all the equipment needed to fill those silos, and I was going broke. In 1988, we had a terrible drought and I had to buy a tremendous amount of feed. It put me in a pretty tight financial situation at that time. My wife and I made a decision about what we had to do. We were going to the bank and telling them we were going to quit. "Then, we heard Dr. Zartman and that was a life-changing experience. After hearing him, my wife and I spent the night at the motel sitting there talking about the possibilities of year-round grazing. We even had breakfast with Dr. Zartman the next morning. At that time I owned about 372 acres. We put the entire farm into rotational grazing. The conversion was fairly simple because I had much of the land in forage. We went from a negative profit to a positive profit very dramatically. In seven years I paid off about a half-a-million dollars. We don't have choppers anymore for chopping silage. We don't need mixing wagons for feeding stored silage. We don't have free-stall barns on the farm anymore. Now, the cows go out and get their feed. They lay in the pastures now. A major forage for us now is orchard grass with a mixture of legumes—clovers and alfalfas. Then we also have a warm season grass called Reed's Canary Grass. We have some fescues. In the winter we grow oats and fescue. We've been doing this since 1991."

But Forgey understood the forces that tended to cause other farmers to turn their backs on the concept of year-round grazing. "The dairy industry," he said, "and the beef industry are highly involved in commercial agriculture equipment and farm supplies from feed, to fertilizer to farm machinery. University research is paid for by industry, and frequently the research is biased toward something in the industry that the funder of the research is trying to promote. The people with power tend to lead. We have a goal on this farm of ours to keep 50 cents of every dollar we take in. The average farm today usually keeps 15 cents of every dollar. Production per year is not what is important, but rather profit per unit. I don't need many suppliers these days. My newest tractor was made in 1984."

Yet despite vigorous, intelligent and persuasive testimony on behalf of year-round grazing, Ohio State University turned down the chance to endorse it as a way to save family farms. My father had faced down numerous reversals of fortune in his life. It was not the first time that one of his visionary crusades had been questioned or doubted, ridiculed or dismissed. He had been criticized and chided for his penchant for restoring old farms, as well. He always moved on, though, fighting the good fight for what he believed in. But this, this failure of the university, the very university at which he had pursued a degree in veterinary medicine, to dare to defy the costly, imbedded conventions of farming that were destroying and driving out family farmers, filled him with despair. He sought only to give farmers a chance to run their farms in such a way that their indebtedness wouldn't keep them pacing the floor in worry and anguish. This, he was trying to do at a time when a study had freshly revealed that the average indebtedness per family farm in Iowa was $135,000.

Dad felt like a man who had been bitten by his own dog. I didn't see it as acutely then as I recall it now, but the academic disinterest and dismissal of his vision of year-round grazing wounded him sufficiently to induce a state of deep personal reflection that none of his family had ever witnessed before.

He had hit the canvas before in his life, and heard the referee begin to count him out. But somehow, he had always risen to finish the fight.

This time was different. The disappointment cut him to the marrow.

"In my heart of hearts I think he was wounded by that," my mother recalled, "and that is when he started pulling away from the university. It was because of the bureaucracy and the big money involved."

He was a little quieter, more introspective. He took it in stride as best he could muster when the phone didn't ring with calls from contemporaries urging him to carry on the fight for year-round grazing. Behind the disappointment was the saddening confirmation of his fear that family farms, disappearing at a stunning rate each year, were taking with them not just a treasured icon of our long history as a nation, but a sacred sanctuary where intrinsic values were being taught, where the catechism of self-reliance was learned anew each day, where children who might otherwise be glued to an X-box in the city were performing chores which instilled a strong sense of self-worth and value to the overall well-being of the family. In my father's daily activities, he would invariably run into friends and acquaintances from the Gallia County farming community and hear from them that their progeny had decided to leave the farming life and southern Ohio to seek opportunities the big cities might offer.

Dad had once said, "All I ever wanted to do in life was make enough money to buy a farm and pay it off full and clear." He knew the importance and value of the lessons that life at the Homestead had taught his children. He was aware that part of the popularity of his restaurants resided in making each customer feel that he was being welcomed to a large farm family table for a good meal.

Dad would continue arguing the case for year-round grazing the rest of his life. But something inside of him knew that he was waging his fight against a colossal, monolithic and startlingly entrenched way of farming. It was perpetuated by those who made fortunes putting farmers into staggering debt and whose tentacles had a stranglehold on every facet of the business.

After my father's passing, Elizabeth Harsh, executive director of the Ohio Cattlemen's Association would tell a reporter, "Bob Evans was committed to helping family farmers by reducing the high cost of making hay with the utilization of year-round grazing programs. His tenacity and personal support of grazing initiatives helped spawn livestock grazing educational efforts throughout the state."

Chapter 10
Chasing Wild Mustangs

The great secret to success is to go through life as a man
who never gets used up.

Albert Schweitzer

A few days before Thanksgiving, 1986, the public relations office of Bob Evans Farms issued a news release announcing that my father, the founder, president and director of the company would resign at year's end.

He left a firm that was posting net sales of $262 million a year. Bob Evans Farms was producing and distributing a wide variety of fresh pork sausage products in 19 states and the District of Columbia, and owned and operated 165 restaurants bearing dad's name.

The man with a million ideas had decided to devote some of that creative vitality on causes about which he had deep concerns—the preservation of the family farm, year-round grazing, protecting this nation's wild horses, conservation and inspiring young people around him. He retired, as he wished, untroubled by second thoughts and unembarrassed by lavish farewell tributes. He had started the Bob Evans Restaurant business with a homely, squat truck stop that served droves of big-rig drivers. He had launched the sausage business in a plant that was approximately the size of a two-car garage, delivering his new product in an old and unrefrigerated truck with sausage that was packed around milk cans filled with ice. He learned the roads of southeastern Ohio backward and forward and became the ruination of West Virginia meat inspectors who regarded him as some *Thunder Road* intruder running bootleg sausage into their beloved state.

His appetite and zest for life were beyond measure. He believed deeply that all that lived was holy, and that he was never closer to heaven than when his boots were planted in a fresh-cut furrow.

My father possessed unfathomable enthusiasms. Dad had a wonderful knack with young people and an unwavering belief in the importance of their nurturing. I secretly believe that they enchanted him endlessly because their minds, their dreams and their wild enthusiasms had not yet been wasted by cynicism, disappointments and disillusion. My father didn't truly retire. He was rather reborn to embrace and champion a banquet of worthy causes that would consume every particle of energy within him. He was never a person who looked down. He was either looking up or looking dead straight ahead. Despite his recurrent heart problems, when he retired at 68, he felt healthy, vital and prepared to take care of some of the business that had been simmering on the back burners.

His six children, who had grown up, quite literally, on a working farm had carved out their own career niches. Stan established a bakery beloved by both commercial clients and everyday shoppers as a Mecca where they could buy some of the finest natural, whole-grain bread products in the Columbus, Ohio. Stephen, after working in sales for Bob Evans, launched a sausage business of his own based in Tennessee. Gwen was part of a husband-wife team that managed a cattle ranch in western Pennsylvania. Debbie became a teacher, marrying a Russian-born coach of ice sports. Bobby sought his fortune in residential and commercial real estate in Bozeman, Montana. As for me, I tried my hand as an air personality in radio for a while before taking a job with a Columbus public relations and advertising firm. With dad's brood making their own way, he was free to turn his energies to causes that had been whispering in his ear for a long time.

He was captivated by the plight in this nation of wild horses whose ancestors had first been brought to the Americas by Christopher Columbus on his second voyage. The Spanish-Barb breed dates back to the era when the invading North African Berbers overran present-day Spain. The conquerors' desert-bred Barb steeds were cross-bred with Iberian horses to produce an animal that would ultimately allow Spanish conquistadors arriving in the Americas to subdue the native peoples. Spanish fortune in the Americas would ultimately wane, but a reminder of their significant presence would remain in the Spanish-Barbs they left behind. Wild bands of those mustangs flourished in the West. Some were captured and bred with horses of native American peoples.

During the Indian Wars, the U.S. Cavalry would commonly shoot the horses on sight, hoping to diminish the number of mounts available to whatever tribe they were trying to conquer and subdue. Wild mustangs from the southeast U.S. were brought west by the Cherokees when they were driven from their homeland along the march known as the Trail of Tears. Widespread slaughter of the mustangs brought them close to the point of extinction toward the end of the 19th century. Ranchers regarded them in much the same manner as coyotes. They resented their regular raids upon grazing lands intended for their cattle, and dealt with them without sympathy.

As a result of a prevailing fear of the unknown history of this breed, many in the U.S. regarded the Spanish-Barb as inferior to native breeds, although it ought be noted that, in 1846, during the Mexican War, a young Army Lt. Ulysses S. Grant rode one into battle. Later, during the Spanish-American War, Teddy Roosevelt led the charge up San Juan Hill atop a Spanish-Barb. Still, ranchers, unwilling to share their cattle-grazing grass with the mustangs, shot them, rounded them up for slaughterhouses or—

according to one report—simply drove them off the edges of cliffs.

Today, wild mustangs (and burros) in 12 western states fall under the protection of the Bureau of Land Management. The present census, according to the BLM, is somewhere around 29,000. Many of that number, however, are not true Spanish-Barb mustangs, but rather hybrids of extensive cross-breeding over the years. There also exists a concentrated herd of wild mustangs in the Virginia-Maryland finger island stretch of Assateague and Chincoteague. According to legend that may be as apocryphal as romantic, the horses of the Atlantic islands are descendants of steeds that swam to shore after a Spanish galleon was shipwrecked off the coastline centuries ago.

Dad's interest in keeping the endangered Spanish-Barbs from extinction actually dated back to several years before he retired. He apparently had come across a story or two about them in horse journals he read and became interested in their plight. When he decided to do something about it, he dispatched a local horse trainer, Bill Wells, to locate what Spanish-Barbs he could find and bring them to Rio Grande where dad could try to increase the herd size.

"To start with," Wells recalled of his first mustang-hunting expedition, "we went out and got a couple of them in New Mexico. Your father had given me a blank check. We got a mare ready to foal and a stud horse. The mare was black. When she foaled, it was a Medicine Hat colt that we named *Este Nacida*, which is Spanish for 'born east.' Sometimes, I would take that colt to the openings of new restaurants. They were a small, hardy horse; a small-headed horse, with heavy muscling, a heavy neck and a pretty deep chest. They had a dorsal stripe on them if they were duns or grullos (silvery grays). They were good endurance horses, but I heard that a lot of ranchers would shoot them because they were taking up their grazing grass."

Dad sent Bill out a second time to fetch Spanish-Barbs along the Nebraska-South Dakota line.

"We got some mares that time," Wells recalled of a jaunt to remote South Dakota and the ranch of an old-timer who had been trying to round up as many Spanish-Barbs as he could keep to prevent them from being shot or becoming dog food or exported as horsemeat and ending up on a dinner plate in one or another of a half-dozen nations where human consumption of horsemeat prevails. A magazine article written after dad began to breed the herd to greater size, indicated, "After purchasing five of the wild Spanish-Barbs…Evans brought them to the farm. They have increased their number to 29. They range freely on the farm, protected from extinction."

At one point, when horses in the eastern U.S. were being stricken with a virulent form of infectious equine anemia, my father gave two of his Spanish-Barb stallions to the managers of the Chincoteague-Assateague wild horse herd in the Chesapeake Bay area. As a token of gratitude, our family was sent a barrel of fresh oysters. Oysters are great, though not routinely farm fare, and the kind folks over on the Chesapeake sent enough for us to eat them for breakfast, lunch and dinner for a good two weeks. We had great fun figuring out how many ways you could prepare fresh oysters.

Today, the U.S. has finally shut down the horsemeat export business operations. At one point, however, 50,000 horses were being slaughtered each year to provide 10,000 tons of prime meat for shipment overseas, according to the United Nations Food and Agricultural Organization.

My father's Spanish-Barbs had the run of the range down in Gallia County. To merely behold the herd charging at a gallop across the high grass invoked the words of mustang lover Peg Cash:

They have run with the eagle and felt the earth of unexplored land
Beneath their hooves.
Their past—forged from the steel of endurance
Their present—built on the heritage of the past.
Their future—guided by the reins of destiny.

It was precisely to assure a future for the Spanish-Barb mustang that my father took up the cause of their struggle to secure a place where they could run and graze without being considered trespassers on land they had roamed for centuries or contemptible freeloaders for eating the prairie grass too near a rancher's land.

It surprised me little when dad became engaged in the cause of preserving Spanish-Barbs. Depending upon the angle of view and the beholder, some would have described my father as a restaurateur or a sausage-maker. Some would have described him as a conservationist, others as a farmer. But he could not have been any of those things or, as it were, all of those, without, at the same time, being a horse lover. He loved and trusted horses in the same manner that he cherished and celebrated youth. Some people, as they age, grow less tolerant and more dismissive of the young. As my father aged, it was just the opposite. He never believed, as the old saying goes, that youth is wasted on the young. Inasmuch as he knew that one of his obligations in life was to serve as a steward of the land, he was likewise convinced that it was his duty to be a mentor to the young. One of the chief instruments of that mentorship was horses.

He knew only too well the significant role horses had played in the lives of his children. He knew also, from being a child whose family lacked the means to afford him the luxury of a horse, that something magical could be made to happen by fulfilling the dreams of youngsters who longed for one. The annual 4H horse giveaway was born of his passion to pair deserving youth with horses.

Once a year in September, beginning in 1977, each of 10 lucky youngsters would be presented with a Quarter Horse weanling in Rio Grande. Each of the 10 was selected from a state within the marketing area of Bob Evans Farms, which meant they traveled to the roundup and presentation from as far away as Missouri and Illinois, Georgia and Delaware. The participating state 4H offices selected a representative after the candidates had been judged on "significant personal achievement," citizenship activities within their community and active involvement in 4H programs. Parental consent was, of course, a necessity, as was the requirement that the family of the youth selected have facilities to care for the animal through at least two years.

The fall roundup began with ten lucky youth accompanied by their parents and state 4H advisors converging on the Homestead on Friday afternoon. After some time spent getting acquainted, those participating would saddle up for a brief ride to the farm shelter house where dinner waited. Following the meal, the families, 4H representatives and each of the state winners would ride to a campsite some five miles distant. Plenty of time was provided for the young people to meet new friends and for their parents to fellowship with one another.

Saturday morning brought the actual roundup in which the young- sters helped drive the weanlings into a corral where state winners would be matched with the horse they had won. The night before, each of the youngsters would have drawn a number from dad's Stetson. Nature and horse sense ruled the day. If a young man or woman had drawn the num- ber three, say, he or she would be awarded the third horse to exit the corral chute. It was a game of chance without losers.

As ten horse trailers departed on Sunday for far flung points on the compass, it was clear that something extraordinary and enchanting had taken place in the lives of ten youngsters who had all gained a horse and a story to one day tell ten sets of grandchildren.

After one fall roundup, the state director of the Indiana 4H wrote my father, praising, "You are truly a leader among men and an example for us all." In truth, my father never thought of himself as a magnanimous bene- factor. It simply made him happy to see young people thrilled in receiving what had been his heart's desire as a child. He knew, also, that providing that horse was going to teach responsibility, self-reliance, confidence and pleasure. It is one thing to give a youngster a gerbil or a puppy and quite another to give him a horse. Once again, the author Michael Korda reminds his readers in the book *Horse People:*

It's hard for most people to develop any kind of intimacy with an animal that weighs a thousand pounds more than you do…You can't pick it up and cuddle with it, like a kitten, or curl up in front of the fire with it, like a dog; for the most part it doesn't stand around moping for you until you come home, and although it will recognize the sound of your voice, it will not as a rule respond to the sound of its name. In short, the horse, though domesticated, remains wild at heart.

I have come to that stage of life where, to spend time with my father, I must now do it through memories of him, by visiting the places he considered special or by going through the photographs that remind me of the way he was. Some of my most treasured photographs capture him among horses—among his Spanish-Barbs or atop one of his favorite mounts on a trail ride. When he was in the saddle, he knew that God was in his heaven and all was well with the world.

Chapter 11
Through Innocent Eyes

Garden Flower

`I will rise before the morning sun*
Quench the thirst of May showers in June
I will plant my footprints deep in the soils
Harvest blood red peonies knee high in bloom

I will befriend the dogwood tree
Gripping firm to these winding trails
I will paint red and gold on blackbird wings
Perched high atop the throne of cattails

I will console the sun with this Stetson hat
Casting shadow to comfort its blaze
I will stare in wonder as the pale horse rides
In fields with bare hands I've made

Anthony Donskov
Grandson

Someone once said that the reason grandparents and grandchildren get along so well is that they have a common enemy in the middle. Truth be told, I believe that because parents are saddled with the task of vaccinating their offspring against misbehavior, irresponsibility, stubbornness, defiance, sloth and incontinence, the relationship is often contentious and adversarial. If parenting is school, grand-parenting is recess. Grandparents are spared the ongoing sparring that often colors the relationship between parent and child. Parents must be ever vigilant. Grandparents get to savor the luxury of being ever indulgent. Grandmothers dispense cookies. Grandfathers hand out advice.

My sister Gwen's son, Bart, remembers my father as a sage ever ready to dispense his opinion or advice on every subject at hand.

"I can tell you how to make a small fortune in the horse business," dad once advised Bart. "Start with a large fortune."

Because Bart grew up on a working cattle ranch and, at one point, seemed destined to make it his life's work, dad would tease him, "You keep messin' with cattle and you'll be scratching a poor man's rear end the rest of your life.

"He was fond of calling me at 7:30 in the morning," Bart remembered. Grandpa would feign astonishment that anyone might still be asleep at that hour. "Hey," Bart would defend, "It's Saturday. It's 7:30. I'm in college. Of course, he had already been up since 4:30 and just wanted to rattle my cage."

With each of his grandchildren, my father became a steady boarder in that rambling rooming house that was their young and growing hearts. Even when his grandchildren were far away, he still occupied that room like some big old lovable, bumbling circus bear who—by remarkable circumstance—had somehow been trained to use the telephone.

"When are you coming home?" he would demand of my daughter Alex, tying up a long-distance line between Rio Grande and Boston College, where Alex was attending school on a soccer scholarship. His mock outrage that one of his kin would have the audacity to move so far away from him had the power to transport my daughter to a garden of memory.

"I missed being at his kitchen table," Alex conceded of those phone calls that brought curmudgeonly affection and left homesickness in its place. "It was a safe place to be." Alex was always very close to her grandfather and that closeness found reciprocity in any manner of ways. She was the grandchild who, at age 10, had written and illustrated a booklet titled "A Walk with Grandpa." It was the tale of a typical weekend visit to Grandma and Grandpa's house in the country.

"Hey, Alex, you want to go for a walk with me?" dad would inquire. "We'll walk to the old white barn and check the Canada geese nests at the pond back there on the way."

"Sure, Grandpa," Alex replied in her booklet's narrative. "Let's go." She had drawn a stick figure of herself, a character wearing a funny grimace beneath a thought bubble in which she frets to herself, "I sure hope Grandpa doesn't bring his clippers."

OK, Alex, I'm ready to go. I've got my clippers just in case we see something that needs a trim."

"We walked and walked until I felt like my feet were going to fall off," little Alex wrote, filling the pages with accompanying stick-figure illustrations of the two of them and their activities in the woods.

"Ah, now wasn't that a nice brisk walk," my father responded in her tale. "I just love being in the out-of-doors. And, the old mother geese look just fine. Now, we'll just trim these dogwood trees. We'll only cut the limbs that cross over each other so we allow the air to get into the trees and keep them healthy. We'll throw the branches into a pile. Maybe, in a few weeks when the wood is good and dry we'll have a wienie roast out here. What do you think, Alex?"

The memories my father engendered in his grandchildren were not of trips to Disney World. They were of forays in the pickup truck down on the farm, up into No Man's Land, with all of them bouncing around in the truck bed amid the shovels and clippers and other instruments of construction and destruction he used on his treks into the hills.

"He exposed all of his grandchildren to the outdoors, to the land," Bart said of dad. "He respected the land tremendously because he knew God wasn't going to make anymore of it."

When his grandchildren were visiting, my father was forever inviting them to go with him, to be by his side when he was tending to most any task on the farm. He had a most engaging manner about him at those times. He would act as if he was embarking upon an epic adventure, a deed of high distinction and prominent interest. Or, maybe, it was just going to be plain fun. He had a wonderful way of making a small and mundane task sound enticing. He used the high drama of a carnival barker to convince his grandchildren that the errand at hand was a not-to-be-missed spectacle of the highest order. That always reminded me of the alluring Robert Frost poem, *The Pasture:*

I'm going out to clean the pasture spring;
I'll only stop to rake the leaves away
And wait to watch the water clear, I may:
I shan't be gone long—You come, too…

And, they always did; go with him on all of his adventures.

"There was one memory I have," my sister Debbie's son Matt recalled of a time when he was only 9 or 10. "Grandpa and I went for a drive around the farm in his pickup truck." It was August, and all of the groundhogs were fat and slow as they beefed up for coming winter and their dormancy. Matt and dad were way back on a country road near Hidden Valley Ranch when, by Matt's recollection, dad saw a groundhog (dad possessed the best set of antennae for spotting wildlife, even while he was driving his truck). The groundhog was 100 yards away on top of a small hill in one of dad's pasture fields.

"Grandpa had a gun rack in his truck," Matt said. "When he saw that groundhog, he stopped the truck and said, 'There's a big one, Matt. They make burrows all over my pasture land. My cattle step in them, break a leg and have to be put down. I've lost some fine Charolais to those rascals."

Then, Matt continued, "Grandpa stepped out of the truck and settled the gun on the top of the hood, just at my eye level. He motioned for me to take the shot. I sighted him in. I had never hunted very much. He was 100 yards away, but I got him. When I lifted him up, I realized I had shot him right under his foreleg and straight through the heart. Grandpa loved to brag on me later to my cousins about that shot."

"I think my grandfather really thought outside the box," my son Max said. "He really believed that people would come to understand that his ideas about year-round grazing did work. The reason year-round grazing didn't work was because no one had the courage to turn his back on John Deere, International Harvester and the other big companies. Year-round grazing is going to have to happen. Unfortunately, he won't be around to see it.

"It pained my grandfather that he was watching the deterioration of rural America and that no one seemed to care about things of intrinsic worth: gumption, work ethic, embracing the struggle. It breaks my heart."

Misha Donskov, my sister Debbie's son, said of his grandfather, "He was passionate about the earth, about year-round grazing, about the outsourcing of American labor. All he wanted was to be able to see the common man live a good life. He was always trying to find a way to help the average farmer," Misha's brother Matt said, "That was a passion of his life, and one that he worked at as long as he lived. He had such a profound effect on so many people. I don't know if I ever had a realization of the magnitude of what he did."

I believe that the unspoken message of my father's presence in his grandchildren's lives was a pretty simple one. It was the old advice that Henry Ford always gave to those who inquired about the most important counsel one could offer a young person about achieving success in life. Ford would invariably answer, "If you think you can do something or, if you think you can't do something, you're right." That was Dad.

"I really respect what he created and the risks he took to do it," Matt said. "He believed that through hard work you could accomplish anything. That was just a reflection of his character."

Horace Greeley once said, "Fame is vapor, popularity an accident, riches take wings. Only one thing endures. That is character." My father may not been able to quote that word for word, but it is what he lived by, what he believed, and tried to impart to his grandchildren. What stuns me when I think about the harmonious connection between dad and his grandchildren is how vastly different his world was from theirs. He was born only 15 years after the Wright brothers made their famous first flight at Kitty Hawk. Most of his grandchildren were not born until after the NASA landing craft Eagle had touched down on the moon. None of the following were part of the world into which my father was born: Television, computers, penicillin, polio vaccine, heart bypass surgery, push-button elevators, CAT scans, fiber optics, contact lenses, talking movies, video games, FM radio, photocopiers, seat belts, air bags, scotch tape, nylon, long-playing records, heart defibrillators, artificial joints, jet engines, rocket engines, bubble gum and cell phones.

I could list 50 labor-saving household devices that simply were unheard of when my father was a boy, another 50 more inventions that improved medicine, extended life, enhanced travel or revolutionized communications. Yet the man born before any of those inventions became reality communicated exceedingly well with young people born after all of them were being taken for granted.

"He always had a high level of intellectual curiosity," Misha said of Dad's unquenchable quest for new information. "He was always looking for better ways to do things, the latest information. He always had a *Wall Street Journal* under one arm, a copy of the latest *Time* and *Newsweek* under the other. He would have his highlighter out.

"He was extremely generous about sharing what he knew or had just learned."

Given my father's belief that each generation was duty-bound to leave the world a little better for the next, I can't say that he was totally pleased with trends that had begun in his era and—carried to extremes—done little to enrich the birthright of his grandchildren. While he believed that most of his generation and the one that followed were instinctively good people, both could be wasteful, unconcerned about conservation and stewardship of the land, prodigal in their consumption of endangered resources and individually unresponsive to their obligation to leave the world a little better place. The legendary Ohio State University football coach Woody Hayes, a friend of my father, was fond of saying, "We weren't put here on this earth just to eat, burp and leave. You can't pay back those people who tried to make your life a little better, so you've got to pay forward."

Dad echoed that quotation about paying forward when he reminded his offspring and their children, "You never drink from the well you dug. You drink from the well you found and dig a new well for the next passerby." Parents pay forward when their children are young through instruction, direction and correction. Often that role becomes contentious, adversarial. Conversely, the manner in which grandparents pay forward is by advising, counseling and sharing. Parents are helmsmen. Grandparents are navigators. The latter have complete freedom in suggesting how to avoid dangerous shoals and how to time the reefing of the sails. That, precisely, is what my father was to his grandchildren. But, he didn't do it alone.

"There would be no Bob Evans without Jewell," Max has said of my parents. "He hit a home run when he got her."

"He loved her above everything else," Alex said. "He was madly, hopelessly in love with her. If my grandmother didn't agree with something, I knew my grandfather wouldn't agree either. It was a simple equation."

One of the paradoxes of my father's role in the lives of his grandchildren is that, although he routinely coached them on trying to be their own people and to be comfortable with the counsel they kept in their moments of solitude, the message they received wasn't necessarily the one he intended.

"I find myself thinking, 'I wonder how my grandfather would have handled this situation,'" Misha says today. "What he really inspired me to do was to be an outside-the-box thinker.

"But when I think of him, I tell myself that he is what I want to be."

Dad with his five-year-old grandson Max at Gallipolis. (circa 1981)

Dad takes part in Grandfather's Day at Cherrington Elementary School in Westerville, Ohio. His niece Morgan Miller is at his left. (Columbus Dispatch photo)

At 88, dad becomes the oldest hunter in Ohio to bag a wild turkey in 2006 with his grandson Bart Kayser in Gallia County, Southern Ohio.

Dad marks his 70th birthday in 1988 at Rio Grande, Ohio. (Columbus Dispatch photo)

Colonel Harlan Sanders, dad's grandson Bart Kayser and dad. (circa 1979)

At Cincinnati Reds Dream Camp in 1987. (Columbus Dispatch photo)

Robbin Evans and dad at home in Ohio. (circa 1995)

Spanish-Barb mustangs running free on Bob Evans Farms, Rio Grande, Ohio.

Dad and mom dance at the Candy Cane Ball, Columbus, Ohio. (circa 1988)

Chapter 12
American Originals:
The Colonel, Dave and Dad

Success is nothing more than doing what you can do well; and doing well whatever you do, without thought of fame.

Henry Wadsworth Longfellow

In 2008, it is quite likely that more young Americans know the words from which the abbreviation KFC was distilled than can name the U.S. president whose name was routinely shortened by the public to JFK. That news may come as a disappointment to some. But, the memory of the architect of a legacy often fades though the legacy lives on. KFC is a household word, even though a steadily diminishing number of consumers are able to put their finger on the name of that old guy with the coiffed pompadour and goatee still smiling benevolently down from a fried-chicken sign.

Colonel Harlan Sanders, the founder of Kentucky Fried Chicken, was good friends with my father, as firm a friend as dad would later become with Wendy's founder R. David Thomas. The connection among the three men is more than incidental, even though Sanders was almost 30 when dad was born, and Dave Thomas did not draw first breath until dad turned 14. The glue that bound this trio was much more than the similar career paths for which most of the public would come to know them. Sure, they all launched restaurant chains endearing them to diners, but the common currents run deeper and date back to the childhood of each.

Fate did not wait for the three to become men before challenging them. At 5, Sanders attended the funeral of his father. His mother, suddenly a widow caring for Harlan, a younger brother and, with a baby on the way, told her oldest that he would be expected to help care for his little brother and the new baby so she could support them. By 11, the boy who one day would be called "The Colonel" had been hired out to help on a farm near his southern Indiana home. The $4-a-month stipend he was paid went to his mother. When she remarried the year he turned 12, he fled a brutish step-father's treatment and took a job as a blacksmith's assistant in a railroad roundhouse. It was 1902.

By 16, he landed a job as a streetcar conductor, a position that lasted only long enough for him to allow a pair of Army recruiters to talk him into lying about his age so he could savor the life of a soldier of fortune. Not quite 17, he found himself shoulder to rump with a shipload of mules headed for recently occupied Cuba. Between the seasickness and the wafted scent of manure, he was ready, by the time he landed, to confess his underage ruse to an Army colonel and be sent home. He sold tires, operated a gas station, even ran a ferry that carried passengers from Jeffersonville, Indiana, across the Ohio River to Louisville. He was operating a gas station that sold farm equipment on the side when the first year of the Depression bankrupted him. He moved his family to Corbin, Ky., a patch of the Bluegrass State known, thanks to bootlegging and violence, as "Hell's Half Acre." There, much like my father 16 years later, he launched a little café to serve travelers motoring along Route 25. He might have been content to do that for the balance of his days, if the pending arrival of the interstate hadn't brought him news that the big new road would bypass his café and motor court. At 65, and facing the prospect of surviving on the diminished proceeds from his auctioned business along with a $150-a-month check from Social Security, he picked himself up, patented his method for pressure-cooking fried chicken and began trying to franchise the idea--with its storied "11 herbs and spices"--to restaurant owners.

Dad's path crossed that of the Colonel at a restaurant trade show, most likely in Chicago. Sanders was going from one food or restaurant convention to another, pressure cookers and pamphlets about his amazing creation packed in the trunk of a Cadillac long past its prime. My father loved to contrast the Sanders of those lean days to the later version my parents ultimately visited at his Kentucky estate during Derby Week. What dad saw in Sanders was the trait that linked the two. He liked the Colonel's capacity for picking himself up after adversity had knocked him on his can, then moving on without so much as a sideways glance over his shoulder. After all, by that point in his life, my father had done the same himself a few times, having been moved five times within his family when he was six years old, and being told by his father to build a machinery shed in case the sausage venture failed. Dad recognized that while the white suit and Rhett-Butler ribbon tie were mere sideshow for the sake of selling chicken, Sanders believed that he had a better way. Dad was persuaded sufficiently to negotiate, with nothing more than a handshake, an arrangement by which Colonel Sanders Kentucky Friend Chicken would be sold from the menu of dad's restaurant and drive-in in Gallipolis. Strange though it sounds today, one of the first restaurants in Ohio to sell KFC did so beneath Bob Evans signage.

The Colonel, moving on from his success at landing the Bob Evans Steak House as a franchisee, found another willing taker at a Ft. Wayne, Ind., restaurant called Hobby House. A Hoosier entrepreneur named Phil Klauss had founded the eatery and operated it successfully for a number of years by the time he bumped into the Colonel at a food show. As with dad, Sanders ran his sales pitch on Klauss, hoping that the man would welcome

Kentucky Fried Chicken into what was already a hugely successful family restaurant. When Klauss departed Ft. Wayne for the show at which chance would lead him to the Colonel, he had left his restaurant to be managed by a former Army mess sergeant named Dave Thomas. Klauss hadn't the slightest compunction about his temporary absence from the business. He knew Thomas was a capable boss and a tireless worker who had been toiling at the business of feeding folks since before he was a teenager.

Although the life of R. David Thomas is one of success beyond measure, its hard scrabble beginnings were anything but auspicious. Like the Colonel, Thomas had witnessed the death of a parent when he was only 5. In Dave's case, it was his adoptive mother Auvela. At the time, the boy did not even know that the woman whose casket he watched lowered into the Tennessee soil had actually been his adoptive mother. The death left him with a father who moved around from job to job, married four times and was about three quarts low on parenting skills. Rex Thomas' relationship with Dave was tempestuous. Dave knew, as do most children who are taught life's hardest lessons first, that if he was going to make something of himself he was going to have to grab a root and growl. His grandmother, Minnie Sinclair, with whom he spent stretches of his childhood, proved an antidote to Rex's inflexible self-absorption. She had reared four children on her own after her husband was killed in a railroad accident. Firm but fair, she established a work ethic in Dave, compelled him to understand the consequences of his behavior, and rewarded him when he took responsibility for his actions.

Like my father, Dave started working early in his youth—carrying newspapers, delivering groceries, setting pins at a bowling alley before the era of automatic pin spotters. Early on, he realized a certain mystique about restaurants that enchanted him. He liked the idea of doing something for the public that left them contented and smiling. He fudged about his age to land a spot behind the soda counter at a Walgreen's. The crisp white shirt, bowtie and paper soda jerk hat suited him fine. He may have been shy, a little out of his element in many venues of his life, but restaurants were not among such places. He had learned that from his Grandma Minnie, who, even after her children were grown, was working as a prep cook at an Augusta, Michigan, restaurant. Her grandson often accompanied her to work, and while she—as all kitchen help—was required to report to work exclusively through the back door, she introduced Dave to a magical environment.

Throughout Thomas' teen years, he was always able to find restaurant work whenever his father packed up his sons and his suitcases to chase another job or wife. It was, thus, not surprising that when Uncle Sam called Dave, the Army discovered that it had an already-trained, capable mess cook and kitchen manager in Pvt. Thomas. Dave regretted leaving his job at the Hobby House, but owner Klauss told him his apron would be waiting for him when he returned. In post-war Germany, Thomas managed an enlisted men's club. When he was handed the assignment, the military bistro was turning only $40 a day in food sales. The profits came from 10-cent-a-shot liquor, but Thomas decided to change that. Like my father and the Colonel, he saw a need and had the vision to make it happen. At first, newly promoted Sgt. Thomas saw his hard work go for naught, as soldiers took their drinking money outside the camp gates to the German "guest houses." By feeding the military police at the main gate for free, Thomas was able to drop the hint that he would sure like to see some of the soldiers' pay being spent inside the base on good food. Thereafter, the MPs would occasionally make a sweep of the guest houses, briefly shutting them down so the troops were forced to at least try Dave's food. In no time, the food sales of the enlisted men's club had shot up to $700 a day.

When Thomas packed his duffel bag and his honorable discharge, Klauss was waiting back at the Hobby House in Ft. Wayne, literally greeting the just-released sergeant at the front door of the establishment with a with a freshly starched apron. Not long after, when Klauss returned from the food convention enthused about the Sander's proposition to put Kentucky Fried Chicken in Hobby House for a paltry start-up fee to cover the pressure cookers and the "secret herbs and spices," along with another nickel for each chicken sold, Thomas was unconvinced the Colonel's chickens would fly. He would later write in his autobiographical *Dave's Way,* "I argued, 'Listen, Phil. Why should we pay this guy a nickel a head when we already have good fried chicken ourselves?'" Thomas' boss told him that the kitchen crew spent the whole of Sunday morning preparing 100 chickens in cast-iron skillets. The Colonel's pressure cookers could save more than three hours prep time and make it possible to keep the item on the menu seven days a week.

The Kentucky Colonel (who was, of course, from Indiana) showed up to teach Thomas his method wearing a swallow-tailed black suit and carrying a gold-capped cane.

"We sat down over a cup of coffee," Dave said, "and he talked to me like an old friend. I've never met a better salesman. When he left, I had a sense this man was going to change my life."

Indeed, the Colonel did. After Sanders began opening up his own free-standing units, he turned to Thomas when a quartet of KFCs in Columbus took a nosedive. Dave turned them around and moved up in the growing chain's corporate hierarchy, but by the late '60s, was ready to try his own hand at things.

One year after my father opened the Chillicothe Bob Evans, Dave Thomas opened the first Wendy's on the fringe of downtown Columbus. Dad had started the Steak House, the Sausage Shop and the Chillicothe restaurant with carefully chosen and deliberately limited menus. Both men believed that you find a niche, as a prospector might find a vein of silver, then work it for all you're worth. Thomas did not expand the menu at Wendy's until the restaurant chain had been open a decade.

Looking back over the lives of the Colonel, Dave and my father, I can see clearly the many similarities in their character and personalities, their approach to business and life, in general. Certainly, there were differences.

While both the Colonel and Dave lost a parent at five, my father had the benefit of growing up in a two-parent household. My grandfather was there to teach dad the importance of an earnest day's work, along with the importance of learning to make decisions for himself early in life. My father knew, even in youth, that his actions could result in either benefits or consequences. That is not to say that my grandfather did not have fun with dad. Stan Evans was not a taskmaster. He loved baseball and often listened to the Cincinnati Reds on the radio with his son. The two had father-son outings together, and when Stan was tied up with the business of his grocery chain, my grandmother was at the ready with lessons of her own.

All three men began working early and, to a certain extent, played a major role in their own rearing. Whether it was paper routes, pin-setting or plowing, all three learned in boyhood that you can't be a wallflower at life's dance, waiting and hoping that opportunity will ask for a waltz.

Examining the lives of this trio of entrepreneurs, I sat down and made a list of the traits they shared. The results may not be a no-fail recipe for success, but it certainly served those three contemporaries in good stead:

Each man learned decision-making at an early age and in a manner that nurtured the growth of a strong work ethic. When the Colonel was a 13-year-old apprentice to a railroad blacksmith, an opportunity arose to better his lot and double his income by taking a job as a locomotive fireman. He wasn't certain that he could handle the backbreaking work demanded by the new job or—if he wasn't up to it—there was any hope that he could resume his apprenticeship. He made the decision to grab hold of chance and go with it. When Dave Thomas, as a young teen, wearied of quitting jobs and relocating as his father hop-scotched from town to town, he told his dad to move on without him, that he intended to rent a sleeping room and cast his lot with the restaurant business. When my father's meager earnings from his paper route left him too often with nothing in his pockets but lint, he captured and sold squab to a restaurant, began raising chickens and rabbits for a farmers' market and sold magazine subscriptions.

All three men were risk-takers, but they calculated the risk before making their move. My father liked to say, "You have to jump a chasm. You can't cross it in two steps." Before Dad leaped that chasm, though, he eye-balled the distance to the other side, drew a take off and landing zone on solid ground, made a few quick test jumps, then went hell-bent for leather. He calculated his jump, knowing that you'd better be right if you were going to jump over the certainty of a dime chasing the possibility of a dollar. There was an absence of hubris in Dad, Dave and the Colonel. They were bold, to be sure, but they were not reckless, petulant or foolhardy.

This trio of men were visionaries. All possessed the capacity to see a need and develop a way to serve it. My father studied a little patch of Eastern Avenue in Gallipolis and realized that, with the steady stream of truckers coming and going at the terminal by the river, those men needed a place to eat. He built it. When he couldn't find good quality sausage, he made his own. The Colonel didn't invent fried chicken anymore than Dave Thomas invented the fast food hamburger, but each invented a superior way of making and serving the product.

Each man possessed an immense natural authority and dignity. Those two ingredients are the taproots of charisma, and they instill subordinates with a compelling desire to perform at the highest level possible. The people who signed on to work for my father, Dave or the Colonel knew the boss was a steadfast, level-headed leader willing to share the harvest his dream with those who helped plant, tend and reap. If you worked for my father, you knew it wasn't just a job, it was a journey, and you could have confidence that the person at the helm was more than capable of negotiating the reefs and shoals that were certain to be part of the voyage. Any of these three men would have made a strong political leader had he chosen to compete in that arena, though none of them was willing to compromise his beliefs for the sake of political expediency.

Each man took advantage of the era into which he was born. The Colonel and Dave were born 50 years apart, but both came into this world at a time of great economic stagnation. When my father was born, the nation was still mired in World War I. When he turned 18, the United States was attempting to lift itself out of the Great Depression. The year Dad celebrated his 21st birthday, the country entered World War II. Yet, despite whatever gloom shadowed their early years, each man realized that even shadows cannot exist unless there is a light somewhere. It was by that light that each of these men invented himself. The self-made man realizes that, sometimes, if you want opportunity to knock you may have to build the door upon which it can. Through hard work, perseverance and ingenuity, the Colonel, Dave and my father etched the beginnings of success. When the Colonel was still a young man and rural electrification only a distant dream, he took advantage of the age by developing a carbide-fueled lighting system for farmers. When the post-war domestic boom, coupled with America's growing love affair with the automobile created a vast road-bound population that needed a good, clean, welcoming place to eat, my father built the Steak House and the drive-in restaurant next to it. In the late 1960s, when it became clear to Dave Thomas that American socio-economic trends and dining preferences were lighting a rocket under the fast-food industry he jumped aboard, carving a unique niche in a business many investors thought was either played out or too fickle to be stable.

Although all three men were shy (the Colonel to less a degree than dad and Dave), all were driven. Each brought a boundless energy and an extraordinary appetite to life's feast. Their subordinates worked so hard and diligently for them because they knew the boss was doing the same. If men such as my father's beloved employees Harold Cregor and Elmer Hill sometimes didn't finish loading the sausage trucks until 9 p.m., they knew that my father would be working at midnight. Moreover, they knew he'd likely be up a time or two in the predawn trying to noodle out the solution to a problem.

Dad, Dave and the Colonel were fanatical about quality. Lest that observation be dismissed as simplistic--it being a given that successful people focus on quality--it must be said that to consistently produce a superior product requires a near-obsessive attention to detail. They believed, as William Foster had once observed, "Quality is never an accident; it is always the result of high intention, sincere effort, intelligent direction and skillful execution; it represents the wise choice of many alternatives." The Colonel could be sent into a rage when he encountered a KFC operation which, through sloth or carelessness, was serving customers a product he considered inferior to his ideal. Dad and Dave were no exceptions, though their style for correcting imperfections or mediocrity was not as demonstrative as that of Sanders. Their tone was a little more reasoned than the Colonel's. They realized that subordinates will reach a mutually beneficial conclusion in a timely manner if they are led to it rather than being driven toward it. Even better, dad knew that employees are apt to correct a problem faster and with greater conviction if they can be made to feel that they are a party to the solution. Looking back over the interviews with my father's contemporaries and trusted subordinates to learn the recipe for his success, I noticed that the common thread knitting the essence of those sessions was the single word *quality.* My father so pursued the ideal of quality that it was foremost in his decision never to franchise a Bob Evans Restaurant. He believed that a company that franchised lowered its standards to those of the least caring and attentive of its franchisees. That is not to say that the Colonel and Dave—both of whom franchised restaurants—were less concerned about quality. It is rather that, of the trio, my father refused to compromise it for the sake of profit.

Though all three men were fundamentally different from one another, each respected the other immensely. Dr. George Wolfe who managed Farm Festival activities at the Homestead for a decade remembered from his tenure the day that Dave Thomas showed up in Rio Grande to seek dad's advice about doing television ads.

"Dave Thomas put your father on a pedestal," Wolfe said, "because of your dad's ability to be so successful in TV commercials. Dave came twice to see him, and both visits were to get coached by your dad on how he could be more effective in his TV ads. Your father basically told Dave that what he needed to do was get a little less serious, a little more humorous and to be himself."

Thomas was an extremely bright man, but there was a certain look he was able to pull off that gave the viewer the impression that he was about 7 seconds behind the rest of the world. Self-deprecation being the basis of all good humor, it worked perfectly.

Wolfe said, "There was a vulnerability about Dave that he was opening up to the world. It worked, and it all came through the coaching of your father."

Each of the three men used their hearts to focus the knowledge that drove them toward their desired goals. In life, any number of character traits may propel one toward his dreams. Greed, the adoration of financial gain or the accumulation of power are all quite capable of driving the individual, though all are hallmarks of self-absorption, willfulness and unchecked pride. Placed on the scales that measure success, solving a problem or filling an unmet need were infinitely more important to dad than the profit or praise that came with success. More than once I heard him say of those who built the proverbial mousetrap purely to fatten the bottom line, "He knows all of the words, but none of the music." To him, such a consuming preoccupation was an unprincipled manner in which to move through life. That is not to say that he was not a horse-trader of the highest order. Being a good horse-trader was a badge of honor where he came from. He loved to leverage a deal he could ink solely on the guarantee that his vision, tenacity, ingenuity and elbow grease would forge mutually beneficial results for all parties to the arrangement. By such bargaining he went into business with the malt shop and, later, the Steak House. He loved to recount episodes, the particulars of which revealed his adroitness at leveraging, not because they suggested a capacity for scamming another man, but rather because he had achieved the ultimate goal of converting a mere business deal into a transaction involving personal trust. It gave him pleasure beyond bounds to know that he had struck an arrangement with nothing to put up for collateral save his will, his wits and his heart. It assured that rather than being beholding to a fiduciary obligation he had recruited a partner in his success. For, if my father was nothing, he was a dreamer—as were Dave and the Colonel—and he realized that getting someone to share that dream made them a partner to it. And, while his leveraged deals were commonly secured with nothing more than a hand-shake, he knew it was a handshake that affirmed that another person had just purchased common stock in his vision.

Chapter 13
"The Great White Way."
Introducing Charolais into
North America

Once before you, the cow is a ponderous bulky beast, the very mass of her...striking fear into the minds of the timid as they see her rise. The most graceful part of the animal is the upper neck, attractive in confirmation, flexible, soft and pleasant to the feel; it is about the neck that one wants to throw the arm, for a cow responds to affection.

Jared Van Wagenen
The Cow

For all of my father's considerable efforts to improve, refine and expand upon cattle breeding in the U.S., from Angus to Brangus to Charolais, his work in that arena might have intrigued his counterparts in Europe and Asia who had been endeavoring to perfect special breeds for centuries before dad was born. The nation that was witness to my father's nativity possessed only one breed of cattle when the Pilgrims first landed at Plymouth Rock. Some 25,000 years before the white man arrived in the

Americas, bison had become a part of the continental habitat by grazing their way east across the land bridge which today is the Bering Straits. The bison were a descendant of the ox-like bovine, the Auroch, depicted in primitive cave etchings in Europe from the hieroglyphics in Lascaux, France to the *Abrigo de los Toros* ("Cave of the Bulls") in Spain. When the Colonies were settled, the prevalent breeds of cattle both for dairy and beef production were British imports—chiefly Hereford, Angus and short-horns.

The Charolais were first introduced into the Americas in 1934 by a Mexican industrialist who had become familiar with the breed when he served as a volunteer with the French Army in World War I. It is one of the oldest of French breeds, believed by many to trace its origins to the inva-sion of France by Romans, who brought their only cattle with them. The breed takes its name from the Charolles region of Central France, where Charolais became dominant after the departure of the Romans. The cattle became popular in the United States in the late 1950s and early 1960s as breeding problems began to surface with more traditional herds. Breeding habits had left traditional varieties heavy on fat and more lightly muscled.

Randy Reed, who was Ohio's state extension beef specialist for four decades, recalls of that era of cattle breeding, "All the British breeds had gotten too small. They were growing too slowly and fattening too quickly, which meant that you might cut a carcass and have 100 pounds of fat that you had to throw away. "Charolais came into this country because of their superior growth and muscle mass. Some of the early Charolais imports could be very difficult to handle because they were nervous. But, that trait was bred out of them. Your father got involved with the Ohio State Charolais Association and was on the board of the International Charolais Association. I probably met him at a show somewhere. Bob always tried to breed to the best bulls in America. He wasn't afraid to spend money on them because he wanted only the best."

Dad knew that one of the problems the French had routinely faced in breeding the Charolais dealt with the size of the calves. One U.S. breeder noted of his French counterparts, "The French did C-sections like the Americans did castration." But such risky procedures in calving could be managed readily on farms where the herd size might only be 50 head. Dad did much in the area of selective breeding to help eliminate such drastic measures in calving.

American Charolais breeders in the 1960s faced an uphill battle in gaining acceptance of the breed whose rise to prominence is sometimes referred to as "The Great White Way." Many of the more traditional stock shows barred Charolais from competition out of old allegiances to more traditional British breeds. To make the point about the superiority of the French breed, an Iowa farm family actually went to the extreme of dyeing a three-quarter Charolais black in order to get past the breed prohibition at the 1972 National Western Stock Show. Big Mac, shown as an Angus, handily walked off with all the honors at the show though, when the trick was unmasked, was compelled to forfeit the title. Still, the masquerade was a huge coup for Charolais breeders attempting to show the superiority of their cattle.

From dad's herd of Charolais at Hidden Valley Ranch, I recall being most impressed with the size of the breed. A yearling heifer was roughly the weight of Steinway concert grand piano, about 1400 pounds. A full-grown Charolais bull weighed easily more than a ton. My sister Gwen's son, Bart Kayser, who worked a cattle ranch in Western Pennsylvania during his college years, remembered, "I worked several summers on grandpa's place while I was in high school. I vaccinated cattle, tattooed them, did general health and maintenance chores, made hay. My grandpa probably had about 300 to 350 head of cattle at the time. He liked the Charolais because of their size and their muscling capacity. He thought they had some genetic advantages that other breeds lacked. He experimented with some Brahma cross, breeding them with Angus to produce the Brangus, but he was really sold on the Charolais. They were a larger framed breed."

"Your dad bought some Charolais directly from France," Reed said. "He would go there, look them over, strike a deal, and then contact the regulatory people at the USDA. When the cattle came from France, they had to be quarantined for a month at an island station in the South Atlantic run by the USDA. They were trying to guard against bringing hoof and mouth disease into the breeding herds of the United States. Even the imported semen of Charolais had to be quarantined until tests could be run to assure that there was no danger of it passing on disease."

Reed recalls dad as being one of the most inquisitive of breeders he had ever encountered. "He would pick my brain all day long. He wanted to absorb every ounce of information he possibly could. I might be conducting a workshop on Charolais nutrition and look out in the audience and there would be your father. He knew that the nutrition of a Charolais cow was extremely critical during breeding season. She was calving and producing milk and all of that was taking a lot out of her. If you didn't keep her nutrition at the highest level possible, she simply wouldn't re-breed. During our years together, your dad and I traveled all over the United States. We went to Australia and New Zealand. He just wanted to look at their operations, just see how they were doing it." At the same time my father was studying cattle breeding practices and ranching techniques in New Zealand and Australia, he was also studying their grazing practices, trying to determine the heartiness of grasses there and their adaptability for grazing in the temperate climate of the Midwest.

"His passion and interest in year-round grazing really took off in the late 1980s and early 1990s," my nephew Bart said. He wanted the grasses to be hearty enough that they could winter over. It was a means of lowering production costs while yielding the highest benefit. He even planted turnips which he would let the Charolais feed upon in early winter because they were an excellent source of protein.

"Your dad believed that year-round grazing was the best way to keep the small- and medium-sized farmer down on the farm," Reed said.

Neal Orth , a longtime cattleman and, today, the Executive Vice President of the American International Charolais Association recalls well dad's involvement with the breed, though Orth's beginnings in cattle had little to do with the Charolais until he went off to college. "I grew up in western Illinois," Orth explained, "on a diversified general farm and cattle operation. We raised Hereford cattle, a small herd of about 50. I did my education at Michigan State University. I was a student employee of the purebred beef cattle center. In the 1960s there, Harlan Richie was a professor in charge of purebred cattle at a time when we were moving from baby beef, smaller-framed cattle, to more efficient, larger-framed, leaner breeds. Harlan Richie led the charge to find bigger cattle of all breeds. The Charolais was the first continental breed brought into the United States, and I saw my first one while I was a student at Michigan State.

"The Charolais had breeding problems because of the size of the calves, but breeders such as your father made a conscientious effort to lower birth weights." A lower birth weight did not translate into a smaller cow when fully mature. It rather eliminated the calving problems that had been ascribed to the Charolais. "In the 1970s," Orth said, "the boom was on for bigger framed cattle and Bob Evans was certainly one of the leaders in helping make history in the beef cattle industry, and he certainly was a part of promoting the breed."

Aware that dad had conducted all sorts of experiments in the crossbreeding of Angus, Brahma, Charolais and Welsh Black cattle, Orth observed, "I think that was a pretty good testament that, for all Bob did in the restaurant business, he was also quite an innovator in cattle breeding. Obviously, he was thinking outside the box in all aspects of his businesses. Your father really made a difference in cattle production during the decades he brought his innovation and vision to raising Charolais."

The American International Charolais Association, at whose helm Orth now stands, was once but one of three small, independent breeders associations in the U.S. In order for the Charolais breed to catch fire in the United States, that trio of fledgling associations had to convince hard-bitten, tradition-bound and admittedly conservative cattle farmers and ranchers that the Charolais breed was really the wave of the future given the genetic decline and the inherent deficiencies of breeds brought to the American Colonies from the British Isles.

During dad's years raising Charolais, the three breeders associations combined under one banner and my father was proud to sit on the board of the new organization. He always liked to pull his weight when asked to do so. I know dad, though, and I know that what was so important to him and what he was able to contribute to the acceptance of the Charolais was by selectively breeding away the concerns regarding calving. This was a problem of enormous proportions for all breeders concerned. And, it was this problem that he aggressively addressed, helped to resolve and to which he contributed his most innovative ideas while he sat on the board.

It was a sad day, indeed, when dad, keeping no man's counsel save his own, decided to disburse the herd at Hidden Valley Ranch only a few years ago. His health was flagging. He wasn't able to be among the cattle as much as he wanted. Too, I think he knew in his heart that he had opened as many frontiers as he could in refining Charolais and raising the visibility and acceptance of the breed.

When those who knew dad at the AICA in Kansas City, saw the sale ad for his Charolais herd, it was akin to seeing a "For Sale" ad for the horse and saddle of a true cowboy.

Quietly, and with no fanfare, an era had passed.

172

Chapter 14

The People's Homestead:
Farm Festival Days

I see a million hills green with crop-yielding trees and a million neat
farm homes snuggled in the hills. These beautiful...farms hold
the hills from Boston to Austin, from Atlanta to Des Moines. The hills of
my vision have farming that fits them and replaces the poor pasture,
the gullies and the abandoned lands that characterize today so large
a part of these hills.

J. Russell Smith

The pioneers who first broke the land so beloved by my father carried
bold hopes and meager possessions to the Ohio country before it was even
a state. The first of them came from France; patricians fleeing the unrest
in Paris only to learn that that they had been sold a bill of goods about a
bountiful cornucopia of milk and honey on the banks of the Ohio River. It
was the proverbial "oceanfront property," swindle, and it left most of the
French 500 stunned by the primitive state in which they found their promised land. Some returned to Paris. Others moved to the comparatively

more sophisticated and developed cities in the eastern seaboard. Those who stayed--and they had to be a hardy lot to do so--felled the timber and cleared the land, cobbling together as good a life as they could along the Ohio's north banks. Their determination and sacrifices would still be celebrated in Gallipolis more than 200 years after their arrival.

The French may have arrived first, but my father never failed to quickly point out that it was the Welsh who built the roads and bridges, the schools and halls of local government. He carried the flag of Wales, ever believing that what the French had built for the sake of mere survival, the Welsh had improved for the ages.

Dad was proud of the cradle of southeastern Ohio that had always been home country to him, and ever-eager to have the rest of the world see it. His early TV commercials were commonly tagged with a y'all-come invitation that a stunning number of people accepted, motoring down Rt. 35 at random times to see the home of the man who made their favorite sausage. They came in such numbers and with such regularity that many of them ended up on the front porch of our home. They came calling to see that farmer from the TV ads. They took the liberty of peeking into the porch windows and poking around the yard when Megan, our boxer, would allow it. Unfortunately, she was very friendly.

Soon the Sausage Shop was completed just in front of the Homestead in a field where I used to work my horse. It was eventually to be called the No. 1 restaurant in the Bob Evans chain. It was built very close to the highway, and customers were told that the Homestead was a private residence. This deterred all of those curiosity seekers for a short while, anyway.

The transition of the Homestead from private abode to public attraction was not an overnight transition. At our home, the patter of little feet was, as often as not, a visitor or ten my father had prevailed upon to join us at the table and survey the land, perhaps linger for a trail ride. Some were business associates or contemporaries who shared his interest in

Charolais or Quarter Horses, conservation or nature. I like to tease that if Will Rogers never met a man he didn't like, Dad never met a man he didn't invite down to the farm.

My father cherished history, most specifically the history of those who first broke the land where his crops ultimately grew and his own cattle grazed. He possessed an affinity with, and an obligation to, the forebears whose graves he decorated with peonies either over at Cadmus or up on Mound Hill. Some had come to the Ohio country to subdue the wilderness, but died secretly grateful to have fought it to a draw and sired enough sons to bear their pall. They were the people who lived in the cabins which, long empty and going to ruin, dad rescued and relocated to a place near the Homestead. He christened the restored village Adamsville in honor of Adam Rickabaugh, founder of the now-vanished hamlet of Adamsville located not far from the Homestead. He wanted there to be such a place because he wanted children to comprehend the tenacity of their ancestors and the tribute that was exacted by life on the frontier. My father always believed that it was much more effective to make a point by *showing* rather than telling. Rather than admonish a child, "You don't know how lucky you have it, today," he thought it more powerful to show them how their ancestors lived without any sermonizing about hardship. He trusted young people to get the message on their own.

Thus it was that the self-invited visitors were able to come to the Homestead and behold for themselves, for instance, the types of cabins in which the first settlers in Gallia County had made their homes. They learned that these structures had to be carefully located. Cabins needed to be high enough so neither drainage nor dampness presented problems, for the floor of the interior was often the dirt on which a cabin was built. A cabin was oriented with an eye toward the natural course of the sun and the direction from which prevailing weather typically arrived. Often, if the structure did not have windows, the door opened to the vista of the crops.

Dr. George Wolfe, who once directed and coordinated tourist activities and special events at the Homestead, recalled of the decade he held that responsibility, beginning in 1977, "During the April to October visitation season, we operated the pioneer village of Adamsville. We had free wagon tours of the farm and a barnyard display of animals for the kids. We had a crafts barn that had 6 to 8 artisans present everyday. There was the farm museum to visit and, for the more active, a canoe livery at which they could put in on Raccoon Creek. We had hourly horseback rides and overnight trail rides twice a week. When people arrived, they could see that this was a working farm. They saw crops in the field, cattle grazing, hay-making, people training horses.

"Your father wanted to share with people who had never grown up on a farm, first of all the value of farming as a part of the growth of America. Second, he wanted them to appreciate the many sacrifices of the small working farmer today, and he wanted to represent that group because he felt he was one of them. The whole idea was to provide a service to the public that would give them a greater appreciation and a sense of value of farm living both from an historic and a small-farmer perspective. He knew that the small farmer faced so many challenges that he had to overcome, and we incorporated that information into our message that the tour guides delivered during wagon tours."

To create Adamsville, Wolfe recalled, "We purchased existing log cabins in Ohio, Kentucky and West Virginia. We would disassemble them and bring them to the farm and reassemble them there."

Experts on log-cabin construction were on hand to tell young people and their parents exactly how each structure had been built, from the hewing to the placement of logs to the chinking and roofing. Adamsville was a huge success. That small re-created settlement offered all manner of historic interpretation and demonstrations throughout the tourist season, though never more abundantly so than during the Farm Festival.

"During the time I was there," Wolfe noted, "for those ten years, the Farm Festival went from an attendance of about 30,000 to about 150,000, maybe 160,000. When I came into it, I had been a college professor, a department head at Rio Grande College. Your father and his board asked me develop a plan to meet the increasing demands of the public. Because of the down-on-the-farm television commercials, people just took Sunday drives to search out this quaint little place they had seen as a TV backdrop, which, of course, was Bob Evans Farms. There was a concern that these people were driving hundreds of miles. They would arrive, get out of their cars, take a look at a cow and the white board fence, then go home. There was a worry that the people dropping in weren't being accommodated and that we needed to make it a more hospitable destination for visitors. I was brought into the equation to draw up a master plan to accommodate visitors. The plan was one your dad and the board adopted, and they asked me to implement it. Your father engaged me to do it. He wasn't too keen on college professors, but I think he saw me as a different hybrid to that.

"We did all kinds of things. At the log cabin village, we had people hewing logs, carving wood. We had blacksmithing demonstrations, rail-splitting and barrel-making. We focused mainly on heritage and the older crafts. There were quilters, weavers and spinners. It was all about skills and crafts that people had drifted away from, and we were able to demonstrate them to the public. Demonstrators were dressed in clothing of the era they represented. We had a steam engine that we brought to the farm to run a sawmill, and there was an architect in Columbus who knew all about them. He was busy with his profession, flying all over the country to do his work, yet he could carve out about six or seven weekends a year to come down and put on the garb of an engineer and run that thing."

Even when the Farm Festival was not in full swing, the Homestead was hosting as many as 18 other public events a year from fishing derbies to 4H horse giveaways. On regular weekends, a pair of tractors, each pulling a wagonload of 35-40 visitors left hourly from Adamsville for a tour of the area.

It was of paramount importance to dad that the farm's historic demonstrations be faithful to history and conducted by people who were enthusiastic about carrying their expertise to the public. Young people who attended the sorghum-making operation, for instance, not only got to see the mule running the cane press, but they were given a start-to-finish explanation of precisely how it was done. They learned that the standing cane had to be stripped and topped. They were told that the juice pressed from the cane was then placed in heated and baffled evaporator pans for cooking down. The unwanted waste from the cooking process—starch and chlorophyll—had to be skimmed from the top of the sorghum to keep the finished product from having a bitter taste. Clarity, viscosity and color are three of the qualities by which finished sorghum is judged, and visitors learned how to study the steadying thickness of the product to decide when it was completed.

"This was a living history," observed Mary Lee Marchi, director of the Gallia County Historical and Genealogical Society. "There are not that many places where families could see this sort of thing being done. So many activities going on at the farm represented another time and another era, a slower time and a slower era. People were able to step back and take it all in at an easy pace. They seemed to adopt a different frame of mind when they arrived. They shifted gears a little. You couldn't go anywhere on the farm without running into people who were just down-home folks, people who had time to visit with you, to talk. You have to understand, I am a ninth-generation Gallia Countian, and my grandchildren are 11th generation. What Gallia County offers to us is just a different lifestyle."

Marchi, a quilter from years back, often exhibited her artistry at the farm amid the cloggers, greased pigs and bluegrass music performed from two separate stages. Often 1400 or so campers spread out over pasture land grazing on sausage sandwiches and watching the border collies demonstrate their amazing talents at herding. Then again, perhaps they had just made the pilgrimage to the Homestead to witness the miracle of chickens in flight.

I suppose that no book chapter on how the Homestead became a tour destination and a living history interpretation site would be complete without those flying chickens. Now, some people will tell you that a chicken does not fly. As a child, I simply thought that chickens had brains the size of peas. Still, though, I recall my father recounting tales from his boyhood in which he was determined to examine the flight capability of the chicken. He conducted his experiments—usually a rainy-day activity—from a hay mow where he and Putzig or one of his other buddies had carried a few reluctant hens. They would loft the birds skyward after the manner of an 8-year-old doing the underhanded heave-ho of a free throw. The winner of this little contest was the boy whose chicken landed farthest from the barn. That game proved to be the genesis behind the great Bob Evans Annual International Chicken Flying Meet.

Any Ohioan who has been a Buckeye for a respectable number of years has probably seen TV news stories or glimpsed newspaper photographs of chickens flying out of old rural-route mailboxes attached to the tops of high posts. Chicken flying is hardly news when placed beside the pronouncements of prime ministers or the price of crude oil, but those meets garnered more free media time than anything that went on at the farm. It was the perfect humorous leavening for TV news when the assignment editor needed something a little light between the freeway crash and the latest drive-by shooting. It was just goofy enough to work.

"My son was asked by your dad to help him develop chickens to fly," Wolfe recalled. His boy, Steve, was 10 years old at the time. "We put a chicken coop atop a hill, and every morning before he went to school, he would walk part of the way up the side of the hill and spread feed." The chickens would tear out of their roost to be the first on the scene and, in their haste, actually became momentarily airborne. The next morning, Wolfe's son would spread the feed a little farther down the hill to try to increase flight time, continuing to work with the chickens as contest time approached.

"This was all your dad's idea," Wolfe said. "We had mailboxes that opened at both ends mounted 10 feet off the ground." Chickens in one of four weight classes would be handed up to a chicken air-traffic flight master who was perched atop a ladder. The flight master would open the back of the mailbox and insert the chicken. A gentle tap with a toilet plunger on the fowl's rump was all that was needed to get the bird out the other end of the box and aloft. Wolfe's son, the trainer, even won the event one year and was interviewed by *PM Magazine.*

A story syndicated by Dow Jones Newswires noted dad's preference for a down-home feel to both the business and festive side of life:

A highlight of the annual stockholders meeting was a sausage fry at his farm, which for many years was also home to the annual International Chicken Flying Meet. Chickens were launched from farm-style mailboxes as crowds numbering in the thousands cheered them on. In 1977, a Japanese blacktail bantam named Kung Flewk doubled the old records by flying into a head wind for 297 feet, 2 inches.

"Chickens like to fly," Mr. Evans told the Washington Post at the 1981 Chicken Flying Games. "When I was a kid we used to throw 'em off the hay mow. Those doggone chickens can fly anywhere."

Dr. Wolfe recalled of his years down on the farms, "I had three children. They will never forget the experience of being raised at Bob Evans Farm. My son stacked hay and ran the canoe livery. My daughter was one of the tour-wagon guides. She drove the tractors. It was a foundation for them, and it gave them a work ethic." Wolfe freely concedes that even today, 20 years removed from managing all things public down on the farm, he still misses the place.

I never hear the tone of wistfulness in the voice of someone who has worked at the farm and lived down in home country that it doesn't touch a respondent chord in me. For, after the cars and campers of visitors to the Farm Festival began heading out for home; after the tents were struck and the artisans began packing up their wares for a drive that might consume hundreds of miles, a quiet would begin settling over the homestead. It would begin again to resemble the place where I was reared.

After I married, I was away from Gallia County in Bolivia and Peru for eight years, and for every week I was away I yearned to know the joy of those who attended the various festivals, trail rides and 4H horse give-aways at the farm. I tried to transfer my love of nature to my transplanted surroundings. Yet, no matter how many times I would set out to hike the ancient Inca trails up the mountainsides of Peru; no matter how often I took in the heart of the splendor at the zenith of my treks in the Andes, I would find myself, at day's end, thinking about home. Most commonly, my mental sojourns home would be set in mid-March, earliest April, with me standing at the lip of a small brook which runs alongside our home. I could pick up the faint scent of the earth thawing beneath my feet. That whiff of home country, that hint of resurrection, was, at once, both subtle and exciting. I used to sense the feel of the thaw, as though a terrestrial current moved up from the earth through the very soles of my feet as I stood sniffing at the faintest of scents riding the lift of the wind. "The world is too much with us, getting and spending we lay waste our powers; little we see of Nature that is ours," Wordsworth wrote. That passage always took me back to spring and to my roots at the Homestead.

Spring also brought with it a change in the weather that transported men back to their boyhood. The treasured coming of the wild turkey hunt turned stubborn, sedentary men into 10-year-old boys as rambunctious, excitable and unmanageable as any child held hostage inside on a rainy day. For weeks before the season opened, my father tortured us as he strode through the house with a tiny, elastic device on his tongue, practicing turkey calls. He sounded, for all the world, like something feral. He intended to come off like a romantically inclined Tom calling his honeys. When he wasn't busy trying to sound like a Tom in need of a hen, he would sit intently listening to audio cassettes enlightening him on *How To Call in a Hen* and *How To Ward off Other Toms*. For a few weeks out of the year, my dad would become a turkey, complete with the requisite pea-sized brain. In another man, it might have concerned me that he was also armed, but dad was a crack shot, a ribbon-honored member of the Greenbrier Military School's rifle team. He had hunted wild game since he was 10. A quail hunter by heart, grouse and pheasant were also high on his list of preferences. But, when the wild turkey began returning to Gallia County in numbers sufficient to command the legalization of hunting once more, they had his undimmed attention and an ardor that bordered on the obsessive.

My father believed that there was an incredible intelligence in the American wild turkey, the fowl whose honor Ben Franklin had sought to immortalize when he suggested it ought to supplant the eagle as a representation of all that was wise and noble about the new republic.

"They're the smartest bird in the wild, on wing, even," my father was fond of saying. "You can get away with fooling them once. But, you'll never get a second chance. They never forget. They are so smart they never make the same mistake twice." Of course, if they were at the business end of dad's rifle, they only had to make a mistake once. I couldn't believe my ears when dad began boasting of the intelligence of a fowl whose cerebrum was smaller than that of the proverbial chicken that crossed the road.

My mother well recalls dad's unbridled glee at the approach of wild turkey season. He had spent years crafting a natural habitat where the wild turkey, long-vanished from Gallia County, felt comfortable in returning. When turkey season arrived, my father would set out for the woods, camouflage make-up slathered over everything not covered by his camouflage hunting clothes. He would hunt with Gallia County Game Warden Ken Tomlinson or Bob Donnett, president of the Gallia County Conservation Club. Sometimes, grandson Bart would accompany him. He returned home from one such outing not long after the wild turkeys returned in sufficient numbers to hunt. Bursting with excitement, he strode into the Homestead to mother's entreaty, "Did you get your turkey, honey?"

"No," he smiled broadly, "but I saw one, and I'll get him next year."

The little cabins of Adamsville and canoe livery represented a portion of dad's home country that he wanted to share with the public. He wanted visitors to take a ride on a wagon pulled by a tractor and hear from their guide how a farm is run today and learn some of the serious problems faced by the small farmer trying to make a living in the late 20th century. The geography of Granny's Branch, the stages upon which cloggers and bluegrass musicians performed, he happily shared with tourists who wanted to know what this farmer from the TV commercials had made of his life. Everything from flying chickens to the outdoor Sunday morning homily, dad did his best to present before the public. All of that was part of the home place that visitors came to enjoy, a place to which they would return again and again. This was the house that Bob built, a site to which hundreds of thousands came every year. But, it represented only a small portion of where Bob's heart lived.

Deep in the woods and the thickets or somewhere up in No Man's Land were those small, tucked-away niches where his heart could reside in contentment and reflection. There was located the portion of the home place that was most truly my father. Inside a mind whose gears never stopped turning, he could sit on a log and behold the turning of the seasons, the cycle of nature. He was quiet then. I believe my father possessed the capacity to hear things grow. The rustle of a nesting quail or the approach of a love struck turkey set the beating of his great heart in pure synchronization with the rhythm of the universe.

Dad never minded surrendering that piece of the home place where people could tap their toes to *Foggy Mountain Breakdown,* taste the yield of the sorghum press, sample the kettle-cooked apple butter, be awed by the nimble produce in quilts turned out by local hands, or ponder the cabins of Adamsville while marveling at the fortitude of the first settlers to the area. All of that, he surrendered, knowing that he still could travel to the woods and be held spellbound by the work of another visionary genius:

Mother Nature.

The poet Wendell Berry said of his own strolls in the wilds, "If I just want to walk, and especially if I need to be consoled, I go down to the lane in front of the house and through the gate and into the woods. What I like about the woods, what is consoling, is that usually nobody is working there, unless you would say God is."

Chapter 15
Once More to the Woods

Wherever you are is home
And the earth is paradise
Wherever you set your feet is holy land...
You don't live off it like a parasite.
You live in it, and it in you,
Or you don't survive.
And that is the only worship of God there is.

Wilfred Pelletier and Ted Poole

Although 80 years is but the blink of infinity's eye, my father's friends and kin from all around came to witness the achievement of his many years upon this earth. The entire town of Gallipolis celebrated the milestone in the riverfront park. Dad was presented with a huge birthday card that appeared to have been signed by the whole town. A reception for my father and mother was held at the French Art Colony, and that affair was followed by a special community theater presentation—dedicated to my parents—of the A.R. Gurney Broadway play, *Love Letters*. Sorting

185

through the cards and letters, my father was delighted to find a note from Elaine Hayden Hairston, the chancellor of the Ohio Board of Regents, on which dad served as a member for 13 years:

Dear Bob, I hear that you have just had a very special event! Happy Birthday! It's not possible that you are 80, for your heart is forever young, your mind still learning and your energy still making life better for the people of Southeastern Ohio.

Bob, it has been such a pleasure to know and work with you. I shall always be grateful to you for your confidence in me as chancellor. It was a great adventure and you are a great friend.

Salutations honoring the benchmark recounted dad's remarkable journey from a one-room schoolhouse in Cadmus to the heady status of becoming a "household word." The chain my father had conceived and developed boasted hundreds of restaurants across the U.S. His crusades on behalf of year-round grazing, conservation, saving the Spanish-Barb mustang and promoting higher education for Appalachian scholars were all well-established by the time his birthday cake marked 80 years. Still, he did not view the attainment of that benchmark as a license to rest and retire from his concerns about the world around him.

"Bob tried to be as physical as he could," my mother said of dad's health after he turned 80, "He would always want to be out doing something. He would get out and work in the yard. He planted, cleaned the banks. But he had congestive heart failure. We would make it back to the house after he had worked, and he would put his head down on the table and try to relax and catch his breath. Then he would want to go back out and do a little more. He never stopped liking the things he enjoyed. He loved to hunt, but he couldn't do all of that walking. He couldn't play golf like he wanted to. We sold our little retirement home in Arizona. He wanted to spend the time we spent there on year-round grazing."

It was as though dad, on the brink of turning 85, came to realize even more acutely the ticking of twin clocks. One was the unrelenting march of time—the toll of the church bell, the blue blink of the digital numbers on the clock radio, the passing hands of the clock on the wall. The other clock, the one that had threatened to quit on him numerous times; the one that had known the deft ministrations of cardiologist and surgeon was the one over which he certainly fretted in private, though mustering a bold front for those he loved.

Dr. Brian Griffin, an Irish-born cardiologist who practiced at the Cleveland Clinic is a man who, quite literally, came to know my father inside and out.

"I got on well with him," Griffin said of dad, "because he was Welsh and I am Irish. We were fellow Celts. He wasn't very fond of the English. I wasn't either. He was a very impressive man who cared about things that very few people cared about. He was very interested in the environment before it was the fashionable thing to do. He was a man who always needed to have something to look forward to—his next project, the next event, his birthday or a family gathering. He needed that to the very end. He wasn't a person caught in the day-to-day. He always had to have something down the road. I think he was a very realistic guy. He knew he was running out of options, but he still had things he wanted to do.

"Everybody who worked with him here at the Cleveland Clinic found him to be an incredibly engaging person. He was very down to earth. In Ireland, we say of such people who made it big but remained unchanged, that he never lost the run of himself. Your dad had a number of different heart problems over the years. He had coronary artery disease and had undergone bypass surgeries. He had a narrowing of the outflow valve of the heart pretty bad. Normally, the heart pumps 50 percent of its blood volume at any time. By the time he came to surgery, he was pumping 20 percent. He was in heart failure.

"We made a decision to operate on him when he was 85. It was a very high risk procedure in an older person, and your father was somebody you had to present something to in a very definite manner. As long as you had good reason on your side, he would listen to you. I explained to him that we would be putting in a new heart valve made of cow tissue. Your dad being your dad, he wanted to know what breed of cow it was. That was his glory."

Mother said, "Your father knew that if he didn't have the surgery, there would be no chance to get well. If he didn't have it, the bouts with faintness and breathlessness would only get worse and he would just pass away."

The surgery consumed the whole of a workday, but dad pulled through. In the first few days that followed, he seemed groggy, almost stunned. Gradually, though, he emerged from that post-surgery haze and began the first steps of cardiac rehabilitation.

"He wanted to live so bad," his cousin Clyde Evans recalled following the surgery, "and he worked so hard to come back. He would go down to Holzer Hospital and work out two or three times a week in the cardiac rehab area."

Once he had regained a measure of his old energy and enthusiasm, dad returned immediately to his campaign for year-round grazing.

"He carried that bone for a long time," mom said. "He would tell me about it, but that was like preaching to the choir. He studied everything he could get his hands on. He sharpened his pencil. He did the numbers on nutrition for cattle and what Mother Nature could provide to take care of the balance."

It was not as though his ego was seeking the achievement of a final masterpiece from life. Nor was it that his life's other triumphs were inconsequential to him. He took great pleasure in the fact that the American dining public had bestowed such favor upon his family restaurants. He considered it no small accomplishment that he had been able to take a sausage he was told he would go broke trying to sell and make it the first choice of consumers wherever people shopped for groceries. It was rather that he knew in his heart that while, in a world suddenly absent of Bob

Evans Restaurants or the many grocery-store products that bore his name, people would find alternatives. For the family farmer in America, though, struggling to keep a head above rising water, the widespread adoption of rotational grazing might be the only chance for survival. It was not an idea requiring budget-busting outlays of tax dollars or the establishment of a massive and unwieldy bureaucracy. It was as simple as sun, soil and seed, as fundamental to nature as making chlorophyll, as stated in Wendell Berry's works.

"My love for the land has always been a driving force in my life," dad had told a reporter for *Land and Water* magazine. "I haven't invented anything new. All I'm trying to do is heal the land with grass, let the cattle harvest their own food and make it possible for small farmers to make a decent living. This system makes it possible for young farmers, who may not be able to afford to buy expensive machinery and equipment, to save money, labor and business. The only equipment you will need is a bush-hog, a tractor and some electric fence."

"There is no one who was more of a confirmed conservationist than Bob," his cousin Clyde said. "It would consume him. He would call sometimes two or three times a day. He may have been the most persistent man I have ever known."

"To the living end," mother said, "he would preach about year-round grazing to anyone who would listen. He was only too happy to stand up at a meeting and talk about it. You might be at a restaurant and he would get you aside and tell you all about it."

He was preaching about an "inconvenient truth" before anyone ever thought it might make a good movie about waking people up to the needs of the earth. He would have driven anywhere to expound upon rotational grazing, but for the small fact that Dr. Griffin had told him that it was no longer wise for him to be driving following the bypass surgery and the valve replacement. As he loosened his grip on the car keys, he would often make the rounds of the county in the company of his friends Bob Donnet and Kenny Tomlinson. Recalling the jaunts of those three musketeers, Donnet said, "We would go to Farm Bureau meetings or to the Gallia County Gun Club. Sometimes, we would just go riding around the countryside." Bob took dad hunting for wild turkey one of the last times my father felt up to going.

"We went up onto his farm," Donnet said. "It was easy walking right there, and there were a lot of turkey. Rowdy and Bart had set up a blind for us. Bob got in there. I was calling the turkeys. I called out several, and I'd signal him to take the shot only to find him asleep."

However, on dad's last trip hunting wild turkey with Bart, he earned the distinction of becoming the oldest man in the State of Ohio to kill a wild turkey in 2006. He was 88.

February, 2007, was less than two weeks old when my father asked Jane, my parents' housekeeper to help him find a local phone number. He was a little weak, but he insisted on dialing the number himself. It was the local florist. As busy as he commonly kept, it had often fallen to Debbie or me to remind him to send flowers on special occasions. In fact, we usually ordered them on his behalf. This time, he negotiated the transaction. It surprised no one so much as my mother when, a day or so later on Valentine's Day, she received an immense arrangement, a rainbow of hues in spectacular contrast to waning winter's gray days. A bouquet from the florist usually carried my father's full name on the card. This time was different.

"Jewell," the message began. "I don't know how I got so lucky. Love, Bob."

It was the most tender of acts from a man often made awkward by open displays of love. I wonder, now, if some premonition was tugging at his sleeve, for, on Feb. 17. a cold Sunday evening, he was sitting at the kitchen table at home when he mumbled to my mother, "Jewell, I can't talk."

Rushed to St. Mary Hospital in Huntington, W.Va., he had suffered a stroke. For five days running, we were told by physicians that he could not possibly survive. But survive he did. His speech was impaired, though, and his smile was crooked from the effects of the stroke on his facial muscles. He ultimately returned to Holzer Hospital to begin physical rehabilitation.

He made his date with the daffodils once more, and was able to conduct a personal inspection of his cherished peonies. He returned to his home April 17. In waning May, with his birthday approaching, the family decided to hold a small party to celebrate his 89th . Nothing lavish. This one was to be family only, an informal cookout at my niece Leigh's cabin up near No Man's Land.

If our children are our chief hedge against our own mortality, then our grandchildren certainly are doubly so. As for the great-grandchildren, they are handed down straight from heaven. Four generations of Evanses gathered to celebrate at Leigh's cabin in the woods, and dad was in his glory. Chief among the adoring grandchildren at his knee was Leigh's 6-year-old daughter, Gwen. We called her Gwennie. Leigh had named her for my sister, Gwen, who had died nine years earlier. Although small children are not uncommonly intimidated by the countenances of their elders, Gwennie had latched onto dad from the very beginning. She could not get close enough to that big old bear with the bristly chin stubble. She was a charmer and a real flirt. We all agreed that the enchantress our sister had been was somehow being channeled through her granddaughter. Dad was in heaven. He smiled a broad smile for the birthday shot.

When I glimpse that photo today, I try to imagine what was going through his mind. The only fortune that had ever mattered to him was huddled at his feet. A day earlier, at home, we had wheeled him out to the breezeway so he could take in the vista of ripening spring in the hills he held so dear.

"I got lucky," he conceded to mother as he took in the view of the flowers and the hummocks of emerald beyond. "I can't get that lucky again."

That thought, that cup brimming with deep gratitude, was wrought in the smile he flashed for the camera on his birthday. "I'm gonna beat this thing," he must have been thinking as he and mother returned home.

That night he fell ill.

Less than a month later, after contracting a staph infection through the intravenous port that had been set up to monitor his blood and administer medications, he died surrounded by family at the Cleveland Clinic.

Newspapers from the *Wall Street Journal* to the *Gallipolis Daily Tribune* chronicled his life's achievements as they noted his passing. Journalists, attempting to describe a mountain range they are beholding for their readers, tend to go for the tallest peaks first. Dad's accomplishments as a restaurateur, entrepreneur and sausage-maker took top billing over the battle he waged for year-round grazing, for better access to higher education for Appalachian scholars, for conservation and stewardship of the land, for his noteworthy successes in breeding and showing Quarter Horses and Charolais cattle, for his attempts to preserve the wild Spanish-Barb mustangs and for championing farm youth and the many causes of 4H.

Ohio Gov. Ted Strickland, noting the passing of a man who had been as much an advocate of the Gallia County area as Strickland had been as a Congressman from his own niche of rural Ohio, called my father a "true original. I've appreciated the opportunity to know Bob personally and greatly admired his wit, his intellectual curiosity and his deep love for his native state."

In his early advertising, dad would commonly end a television commercial by reminding viewers of the product he was selling: "Made by a farmer on the farm." That, pure and undiluted, was my father.

People believed him. They should have. In 89 years of living his word had always been his bond, his handshake better than any contract drawn up by a blue-chip lawyer. He was always just Bob, a farmer down on the farm.

Chapter 16
Laurels and Accolades

To laugh often and much. To win the respect of intelligent people and the affection of children. To earn the appreciation of honest critics, and endure the betrayal of false friends. To appreciate beauty, to find the best in others, to leave the world a bit better whether by a healthy child, a garden patch, or a redeemed social condition; to know even one life has breathed easier because you lived; this is to have succeeded.

Ralph Waldo Emerson

It should little surprise anyone that a life as full as my father's should have required two commemorations to note its end. When dad was returned to his cherished Gallia County following his death, the Lyne Center at The University of Rio Grande was required to accommodate the crowd which came to bid him farewell. A harp and an oboe near the banked floral sprays opened the service with the Quaker hymn *Simple Gifts*. As the music played, veterans of various branches of the armed services approached the peony strewn casket and, drawing themselves up to attention, offered a final salute to dad. American and Welsh flags honored both his heritage and his service to his country. Not far away, one of dad's familiar blue blazers hung from a hat rack crowned by a white Stetson and a black string tie.

Following the invocation of Pastor John Jackson, my nephew Anthony approached the pulpit to offer his thanks to dad for the gift of his mother. A young man of few, but eloquent words, he introduced a song he had written to say goodbye to his grandpa. The tune he had crafted was beautiful for both its lyrics and soulful melody, and profoundly insightful in its recognition of dad's natural reluctance about flamboyant demonstrations of affection. Dad, after all, was a cowboy, and as the title of Anthony's song reminded the mourners, *Real Cowboys Don't Cry.*

So count these wrinkles as memories,
And count these scars where pain used to be.

The song said all that was needed to be said about where dad had been and where he was headed:

I'm as free as the red-winged blackbird
My soul's right where it should be.

My brother Bobby recalled for those assembled, "My dad first took me to Montana when I was still a boy. There, I was aware of his connection with the land and the people."

Bobby spoke of how my father's abiding respect for the land translated so readily into his passion for the causes of conservation, year-round grazing and 4H. "God must be a cowboy," he concluded. "We know today that my father is saddled up and riding the range under the big sky."

Neither the funeral service following dad's death nor the celebration of life that followed it two weeks later were bereft of humor. It, after all, would have been uncharacteristic for a commemoration of my father's life to exclude the more playful side of dad.

The pastor at the funeral service, while acknowledging the many who had come to honor dad in the name of agriculture and conservation, pointedly noted, "I don't see anybody here from the highway patrol. When Bob quit driving, they all must have retired." He followed that quip with the oft-told tale about dad being stopped by a highway patrolman near Jackson while on his way up to the corporate offices in Columbus. As the young officer scribbled out the ticket, dad suggested, "You might as well write out two, because I'll be coming back this way later today."

While the speakers at the funeral service were largely friends and family, those who assembled for the celebration of life at The Ohio State University's Mershon Auditorium, several days later, addressed one or another aspect of dad's professional or avocational passions which had brought their paths together. At Mershon, he was saluted for his work in the founding of the Ohio Appalachian Center for Higher Education. It was noted that his face was one of the first to grace a billboard for the "I am a child of Appalachia" campaign of the Foundation for Appalachian Ohio.

The Rev. Richard Ellsworth opened the celebration of life by remarking, "O God, we gather here today to celebrate the many stepping stones Bob Evans placed for others." Jim Helt, an Ohio State University development officer who worked extensively with 4H throughout the state recalled that dad placed many of his "stepping stones" in the paths of youngsters who were members of 4H. Dad's philanthropy included scholarships, camp and conservation projects, the Ohio State Fair market pig auction, along with the quarter-million dollar challenge grant that helped Canter's Cave 4H Camp construct the Elizabeth L. Evans Outdoor Education Center.

Steve Davis, the current chairman of the board and CEO of Bob Evans Farms, Inc., noted of my father, though long absent from corporate headquarters, "Bob's invisible hand continues to guide us." Davis talked about traveling to Gallia County to meet with dad, smiling as he noted that my father had already assembled a "Steve Davis file" on him. Speaking of my dad's beginnings in the restaurant business, he said of my father, "If he hadn't had this idea many years ago, I would not be here today."

The final speaker at the Mershon gathering was Harold Cregor. I thought it altogether fitting that the first employee my father ever hired, and the dearest of his friends, should go last. Making his way to the lectern, Harold paused for a heavy moment, looking up at the image of dad projected on a screen behind the speakers, then saluted. It was a gesture that spoke volumes about what the two men had meant to one another.

At the funeral service at Rio Grande, the pastor chose a Psalm for his reading from the Bible, though it was not the most famous and widely recited one. Instead of the 23rd Psalm, he selected the 24th :

The earth is the Lord's and the fullness thereof; the world, and they that dwell therein.

For he hath founded it upon the seas and established it upon the floods.

Who shall ascend into the hill of the Lord? Or, who shall stand in his holy place?

He that hath clean hands and a pure heart; who hath not lifted up his soul unto vanity, nor sworn deceitfully.

He shall receive the blessing from the Lord, and righteousness from the God of his salvation.

My sister Debbie, quoting from *A Father's Book of Wisdom*, noted, "One of the greatest gifts a father can give his children is to love their mother." Dad gave abundantly of that gift, accepting in return all the love, generosity, counsel and tenderness that were so much the hallmark of mom.

When the service had ended, when the harp and oboe had gone from silence to sound then silence once more, we climbed into the waiting limousine for the ride up to the top of Mound Hill Cemetery and the spot where the earth had been hollowed so my father could take his place among the most permanent of family reunions. We had wept and we hugged one another, for the immensity of loss was too great to get our arms around. We had to hold onto something, someone.

"The service was beautiful," my daughter Alex said, "but it was hard to share that time. I just wanted to be alone with him, with his casket, just wished I had that time"

As the procession passed the Village of Rio Grande's tiny, rural version of fire protection, a pair of volunteers standing beside a rescue truck that sported an unfurled Welsh flag drew themselves up to attention and saluted the passing casket. As we approached the college's athletic fields, where a summer soccer camp was in full swing, boys paused, standing in silent homage as the procession passed.

As the hearse began to draw near the Homestead and the Sausage Shop, the entire road was lined with employees who held signs saluting, "We will miss you Mr. Evans." They stood in silence bearing testament to their loss. As we approached the Homestead, standing in the yard, not far away, a riderless horse—the first 4H weanling my father had ever given away—stood by in honor of dad. As we turned by the craft barn, a new and glistening Bob Evans tractor trailer from the company's fleet of 18-wheelers was parked in tribute to my father.

From Mound Hill Cemetery, the view of the countryside and the lazy curl of the Ohio River was postcard perfect. The pastor recited prayers of committal. At Christian funerals, the soil removed from the hollowed grave is not returned until the last mourner has departed. At traditional Jewish funerals, ritual dictates that each of the bereaved shovel a spadeful of dirt upon the lowered casket. How apropos to the passion of my father's life it would have been to let each mourner who had come to bid him adieu return a few handfuls of Gallia County to its proudest son.

By ones and twos, the bereaved made their way back to their cars. Hours after the service, though, my son and daughter lingered at the grave. Late-arriving mourners found their way to the grave right up through the dimming of the day—a politician from town who knew dad well, a farmer whose chief affiliation with my father had been through the imprint of dad's creed and convictions regarding agriculture. For both men it was simply a small way of seeing dad home.

Condolences arrived from all quarters and brought reflections on his great successes, but also upon his common touch. One such person, Dannie Crothers, had been a classmate of my sister Debbie and the son of dad's first short-order cook at the first Sausage Shop.

Dannie wrote, "Debbie: Do you remember long ago in Mrs. Brannon's first- and second-grade classes when we planted seeds in our little cups of potted soil? The roots went down and the sprouts grew upward and none of us knew how or why? But, in the end, the plant completed its life cycle and died. And, like your father, so shall we. Such is the nature of things. Your father lived a full and purposeful life. Any man would envy his enormous success in business which is not to be overshadowed by his equally great success in his roles of husband, father, neighbor, citizen and humble servant. His legacy and fingerprints on this good earth will live on after our own passing.

"I was saddened to hear of your dad's passing. Our deepest sympathies go out to you and your family. Regretfully, I was unable to attend the funeral and pay my respects to a truly great man. However, I did stop by your old Homestead the following week. As I sat out on the front porch, I reflected back over a time long ago before his fame, notoriety and enormous business success. It brought back memories from a long time ago in the early '60s. You were probably unaware, but your father gave my mother a job following my father's debilitating and disabling heart attack. Your father, in effect, saved us from destitution, and I have never lost sight of this great act of compassion. Also, during my first two years of high school, I worked at Wade Evans' service station in Rio Grande during school weeknights and weekends. I would often service your father's vehicles as well as washing what seemed to be a never-ending parade of sausage delivery trucks. It was hard to balance school work, participate in athletics and earn my own keep. When your father would come around, and when Wade wasn't looking, your dad would often sneak a dollar in my rear pocket. Back then, a dollar meant that I could buy school lunches for a week or maybe cover half the cost of a pair of jeans. He never said anything, but I could see a twinkle in his eye, and I sensed that he was empathetic with what hard work was all about.

"I've always felt a connection with your dad for the kindness and generosity that he showed for me. Over the years, I have often boasted to many of my business associates that I knew your father back before his enormous business success. Anyone who has lived in and around southern Ohio over the past 50 years or so can lay claim in some small part to your father. He has touched the lives of thousands of individuals in a positive way as well as performing immeasurable acts of common good. In closing, the honor and privilege of crossing paths with your father many years ago even in such a small way was all mine. I've not been in awe of very many men throughout my life, but of the few that there were, your father was at the top of the heap. He was a hero and an inspiration to many of us. Rest assured that there are thousands quietly sharing your loss all the while celebrating his great life. Blessings to you and your family, Dan Crothers."

For those of us closest to my father, came the dawning recognition that we would now be compelled to see him with two sets of eyes. Our vision of him as a tangible presence as close as touching blinked closed when his great heart gave out. At that instant, another set of eyes opened. They opened to the legacy of his life, his achievements, to even the smallest of anecdotes which—alive now only in memory—still carried the power to make us sigh or laugh or weep.

When I close my eyes, no matter where on this earth I may lay my head, I can summon forth with stunning clarity a summer day in 1978 and a trail ride shared by no one but dad and me. At the time, he was recuperating from heart bypass surgery, a procedure most men would have regarded as a grave intimation of their ultimate mortality. Inscrutable about the impact of the medical salvo that had just been fired across his bow, he saddled up a buckskin mare as I did likewise with a sorrel gelding, and we headed out for No Man's Land. How many times had the family seen his pickup go bouncing off toward that special niche of terrain, taking note of the time so as to gauge the length of his absence should the need arise to organize a search party. We swore to one another that we would, as a result of his heedless abandon, one day find him beneath his overturned truck near some gully.

That summer must have been a wet one, for the goldenrod was so high that the horses, passing through it, crooked back their necks as though fording a deep saffron river. We must have ridden for a couple hours because, when it came time to turn our horses back toward home, we weren't far from the crest of a hill looking out over what seems like the whole of Gallia County. At the crown of that prominence, a small Baptist church looks out on the vista. It is a country simple place, the churchyard dotted with graves of the faithful, all facing east in deference to the Good Book's assurance that the Lord will come again from that compass point. I suppose that a thousand sermons have been invoked from the pulpit of that little place, though nothing the Bible has to say inside the church is as breathtaking as what God has wrought outside of it. My father took all of it in as we stopped our horses along the trail to sit and pluck a few wild pears from waiting stems above us. We sat and chatted on horseback about the state of the world, and from where we sat that day it looked pretty hopeful. Later, down the hill a ways from the church, he and I stopped again to rest the horses. Dismounting, he knelt where the trickle from an underground spring had cut a small gully down the hill. Wrapping his big, square, paw-like hand around a large stone, he pulled it back and produced from the hollow beneath it, a speckled tin cup, pronouncing as he did, "A little secret only I know. Now you know it, too." He rinsed out the cup and we drank the sweet, clear water before turning the horses toward home.

If memory has flavor, it is sharp and crisp, the taste of wild pear. It is, as well, clear and sweet, like water from a spring so constant and deep and never ending as to mock even death itself.

Dad would like that story. I must remember to remind him of that day.

Lifetime Achievements

1969

Ohio Soil Conservationist of the Year

Ohio Wildlife Conservationist of the Year

1970

Soil Conservationist of the Year (League of Ohio Sportsmen)

Distinguished Service Award (Gallia County Soil & Conservation District)

Appointed to the National Cattle Industry Advisory Committee by U.S. Secretary of Agriculture, Clifford Hardin

1971

Ohio Conservationist of the Year

1972

Bald Eagle Award (League of Ohio Sportsmen)

Ohio Wildlife Conservationist of the Year (as honored by the National Wildlife Federation and Ohio Gov. John Gilligan)

1973

Ohio Business Tourism Award (for educational attractions)

1975

Conservationist of the Year (Central Ohio Anglers and Hunters)

1976

Inducted into the Ohio State Fair Hall of Fame by Gov. James Rhodes

Named Honorary Governor of Ohio

Presented with the Ohio Governor's Award

Received the Ohio Wildlife Council Award

1977

Appointed to the Ohio Board of Regents

1978

Ohio Governor's Award

Ohio Conservationist of the Year Award
(Ohio Department of Natural Resources)

1979

Wildlife Council Service Award (Ohio Department of Natural Resources)

Ohio Wildlife Conservationist of the year

1980

Ohio Wildlife Habitat Conservationist of the Year
(National Wildlife Federation)

1981

Ambassador of Natural Resources (Appointed by Ohio Gov. James Rhodes)

Named Honorary Commander in Chief of the International Chicken
Flying Contest for the State of Ohio.

1985

National Friend of Extension Agents Award

1986

Man of the Year (Ohio Woods & Waters Club of Cleveland)

1987

Inducted into the Central Ohio Business Hall of Fame

Received Soil Conservation of the Year Award from the National Wildlife Federation

Presented with the Wildlife Conservationist of the Year Award from the National Wildlife Federation

1988

The Ohio State University Distinguished Service Award

1989

Ohio Conservation Hall of Fame

1995

National Welsh-American Man of the Year
(Honored at the Waldorf Astoria in New York City)

1996

Presented the Ohio Appalachian Center for Higher Education Award by the Ohio Board of Regents

George Jones Award for Outstanding Lifetime Achievement by a Welsh-American (Green Mountain College, Vermont)

1999

Agripeneur Award (Ohio's first recipient of this honor)

2005

Received 33rd Degree Mason Award, Rufus Putnam Award for Distinguished Service (bestowed by Grand Lodge of Free and Accepted Masons of Ohio, Blue Lodge)

2006

Honorary Director of Agriculture for the State of Ohio

Honorary West Virginian

2007

Bob Evans, only Ohioan to be honored three times by the
National Wildlife Federation

2008

National Humanitarian Award
(Appalachian Regional Commission posthumous presentation to the
Evans family in honor of Bob's achievements for the region of
Ohio Appalachia and its youth)